Tina Houser's

Hiding the Word in My Heart

Fun ways to memorize the Scriptures

Warner Press, Inc
Warner Press and "WP" logo are trademarks of Warner Press, Inc

Hiding the Word in My Heart – Fun Ways to Memorize the Scriptures
Written by Tina Houser

Requests for information should be sent to:
Warner Press Inc
1201 East Fifth Street
P.O. Box 2499
Anderson, IN 46012
www.warnerpress.org

Editors: Karen Rhodes and Robin Fogle
Cover: Curtis Corzine
Designer: Christian Elden

ISBN: 978-159317-752-2

Printed in USA

Table of Contents

PART 1

PART 2

PART 3

Introduction to the Holy Habit of Scripture Memorization

Welcome to the World of Scripture Memorization!

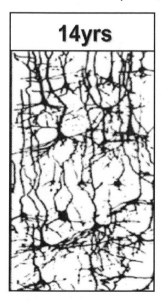

Information I gleaned from Dr. Harry Chugani, renowned for his work in the field of brain research, took my attitude toward helping kids establish holy habits from lackadaisical to desperate. When presented with 3 pictures that depicted the brain's development, it became quite clear to me that spiritual disciplines need not only to be understood, but they need to have PURPOSE in a child's life before the age of 12.

The first picture here, from Chugani, is of a newborn's brain. The lines depict neuropaths that are forming, because the child is taking in information. I think we all can easily understand what this depicts. The child is learning about his or her world.

That same child's brain at the age of 6 looks quite different. It is an accepted fact that during this 3-year period—3 through 5 years old—a child takes in more information than in any other 3-year period in his or her life. Neuropaths are developed like crazy! This is a picture of that same child's brain at the age of 6.

At the age of 14, we would expect the picture to be absolutely filled with neuropaths, almost blacking out the picture. But that's not what we see. Something very interesting happens around the age of 12. This picture depicts that same child's brain at the age of 14.

Around the age of 12, the brain begins something that it will continue through life. It's called "synaptic pruning." Synaptic pruning is when weaker links are deleted. They're eliminated or pruned. (Picture how you prune off the dead branches of a bush.) The stronger connections are kept, so they can strengthen.

So, what determines a weak connection? PURPOSE. When a connection has a PURPOSE in the person's life, it is perceived as important or strong, and is not the recipient of the pruning process. If it doesn't have a PURPOSE—if the brain doesn't perceive specific information as useful—it's pruned.

Why did this make me desperate to instill holy habits in kids before they reach the age of 12? Well, here's why. If we teach kids about Scripture memorization and every week we present them with another verse that they supposedly memorize, but they never view it as important or never use it in their lives in a practical way—if it never is viewed by the brain as having a PURPOSE—then, when pruning time comes, it will be eliminated. That's a scary thought to me! We've got to make this holy habit something that kids are committed to on a regular basis and that they view as being part of who they are. We've got to make sure Scripture memorization has PURPOSE in their lives! We've got to get desperate!

Chugani, Harry T. "Biological Basis of Emotions: Brain Systems and Brain Development." Pediatrics: *Official Journal of the American Academy of Pediatrics* (1998): 1225.

Why Memorize Scripture?

2 TIMOTHY 3:15-17 (NLT)

You have been taught the holy Scriptures from childhood, and they have given you the wisdom to receive the salvation that comes by trusting in Christ Jesus. All Scripture is inspired by God and useful to teach us what is true and to make us realize what is wrong in our lives. It corrects us when we are wrong and teaches us to do what is right. God uses it to prepare and equip his people to do every good work.

If people are very legalistic in their faith and addicted to a "To-Do" list, then memorizing Scripture might be something they do "because they're supposed to." But there are great benefits to memorizing Scripture. Most of them you can't begin to understand until you've immersed yourself in the process. There are special moments when you realize its value… like when you're troubled and your mind immediately goes to Scripture that is hidden inside you, or when you lack assurance and God's promises assure you. Scripture is only able to do that because you know what they are.

Let's just take a few moments to look at what God's Word says are the benefits of memorizing Scripture.

Arms against temptation

(Psalm 119:11, NLT) *I have hidden your word in my heart, that I might not sin against you.*

(Ephesians 6:13 and 17, NLT) *Therefore, put on every piece of God's armor so you will be able to resist the enemy in the time of evil. Then after the battle you will still be standing firm…. Put on salvation as your helmet, and take the sword of the Spirit, which is the word of God.*

Scripture memorization is a weapon. It's one of the weapons that we can pull out to slay Satan. Jesus did exactly that when Satan confronted Him in the wilderness. With each temptation, Jesus referred to Scripture for guidance and His defense. You are not alone to fight against temptation. When you question whether something is right or wrong to continue doing, then Scripture can guide you away from the temptation. But it can't do that if you don't know it!

Helps in processing problems and solutions

(1 Chronicles 29:17, NLT) *I know, my God, that you examine our hearts and rejoice when you find integrity there. You know I have done all this with good motives, and I have watched your people offer their gifts willingly and joyously.*

Scripture instructs us as to what actions God wants us to take. When we know Scripture by heart, then the road of integrity is easier to walk down. When God looks at our hearts, we want Him to find good motives there, and if our decisions and problem solving are based on the Scriptures that are within us, then God will find integrity there.

Provides a way to pray

(1 John 5:14, NLT) *And we are confident that he hears us whenever we ask for anything that pleases him.*

The Word of God is full of His promises. When we pray we can claim those promises…if we know them. I don't know about you, but this is what happens to me. (I think it probably happens to you too.) I learn something, and I can repeat it, but it hasn't reached a place of really meaning something personal. Then, something happens and I need that information. Calling upon it and putting it into action changes how I value it. It's that way with praying Scripture. I learn it and then one day, it fits exactly what I'm trying to express. I pray it out loud and it means so much more than ever before, because it has touched a personal experience and helped me pray.

When we don't know what words to pray, knowing Scripture gives us a voice. It's a way that the Holy Spirit guides us when we can't express ourselves. Again, that guidance isn't available if you don't have the Scriptures in you.

(Romans 8:26, NLT) *And the Holy Spirit helps us in our weakness. For example, we don't know what God wants us to pray for. But the Holy Spirit prays for us with groanings that cannot be expressed in words.*

There are a couple of things to keep in mind when praying Scripture that will make it more meaningful.

Substitute with "I", "my", "mine", and "me" whenever possible in the Scripture to make it more personal. The child will understand that God's Word is truly written to them personally.

Throughout the Scripture, substitute the person's name who you are praying for. This puts a name and face to what God is saying.

Address God personally. Instead of saying, "The Lord is my shepherd", say, "You are my shepherd, God."

Say the Scripture out loud. Doing this defines each word and it doesn't just flit through your brain.

When there is a lack of understanding, pray Proverbs 3:5 (*THE MESSAGE*), *Trust God from the bottom of your heart, don't try to figure out everything on your own.*

When you need help, pray Hebrews 4:16 (NLT), *Let us come boldly to the throne of our gracious God. There we will receive his mercy, and we will find grace to help us when we need it most.*

When someone has done wrong against you and you're having a difficult time forgiving him or her, pray Luke 6:37 (NLT), *Do not judge others, and you will not be judged. Do not condemn others, or it will all come back against you. Forgive others, and you will be forgiven.*

Becomes a tool for witnessing

Scriptures like Romans 3:23, (NLT) *For all have sinned and fall short of God's glorious standard,* are there to aid you when trying to explain God's plan of salvation. You can call on these verses as confirmation of what you're saying, and knowing them shows others that you're serious about your belief in God's Word.

Provides a way to meditate

As you memorize Scripture, there's no getting around the fact that you have to say it over and over again. You have to come back and review it. One of the best tools for memorizing is getting to know the Scripture, understanding the context, and embracing the importance of specific phrases. Each one of those becomes part of meditating and once the Scripture is memorized you have a totally new understanding and relationship with it.

Read through this passage and be amazed at how many different facets there are to meditate upon. Colossians 3:12-13 (NLT), *Since God chose you to be the holy people he loves, you must clothe yourselves with tenderhearted mercy, kindness, humility, gentleness, and patience. Make allowance for each other's faults, and forgive anyone who offends you. Remember, the Lord forgave you, so you must forgive others.*

Strengthens personal faith

When I memorize Scripture, I can't help but learn more about the God I serve. I can't help but more fully understand the people of faith that it tells me about. I can't help but be challenged to raise the bar on my spiritual walk. My personal faith is strengthened. I cannot go unchanged.

(Hebrews 6:18, NLT) *So God has given us both his promise and his oath. These two things are unchangeable because it is impossible for God to lie. Therefore, we who have fled to him for refuge can have great confidence as we hold to the hope that lies before us.*

Offers encouragement

There are verses that encourage me when God knows I need His encouragement. His Word is one of the main ways God makes Himself known to us, and if we don't know it, He can't provide the encouragement we need. There is the encouragement that He will walk with us, that He will be faithful to never leave us, and the ultimate encouragement that there is an eternity to spend with Him.

Hebrews 3:14, (NLT) *For if we are faithful to the end, trusting God just as firmly as when we first believed, we will share in all that belongs to Christ.*

Allows the Holy Spirit to speak

Memorizing Scripture gives voice to the Spirit. It's more than a warm fuzzy feeling. It's words of instruction…or reprimand…or encouragement…or understanding…or assurance—things that the Holy Spirit wants to communicate with us at a particular time. The Word of God is personal. It's a personal letter to you that the Holy Spirit uses.

1 Corinthians 2:10 (NLT) *But it was to us that God revealed these things by his Spirit. For his Spirit searches out everything and shows us God's deep secrets.*

Today is always a good day to start!

Notes:

_____

_____

_____

_____

_____

_____

_____

Keys to Memorization

Now you know why it is important to memorize Scripture, but how do you begin? The following 14 Keys to Memorization are designed to help you overcome common road-blocks to remembering Scripture. They will also help you learn Scripture accurately, help you retain what you have memorized, and identify the type of memorization techniques that will work best with your learning strengths. Use these tips to help you remember God's Word not just for a week, but for a lifetime!

Key #1

Get It Right

A caution when memorizing Scripture: you can't just "get the idea." When memorizing other subjects, often it's good enough to "get the idea" or "get close." You can't do that with the Word of God when you are hiding it in your mind.

You must learn each verse word-for-word. **Close enough is not good enough!** Get it right. Once you change one word, and say it several times that way, it's difficult to break that habit. It also gets easier to replace another word and another. When you do that, you're altering the Word of God, and I know you don't want to do that. Re-memorizing a Scripture is really difficult when you've already committed it to long-term memory.

An excellent idea when you are beginning on the memorization process with a specific passage is to give the Scripture card to someone and let that person listen to you. He or she can point out words you left out, phrases you switched, or new words you've used instead of the right ones. It's wise to highlight those troubling words that you want to stray from. You may not even realize you've been learning it incorrectly, so the highlighting flashes a caution light.

Key #2

Link the Scripture to Something You Already Understand

Through motions.

If you determine the motions that kids are going to use to represent words in the Scripture, they're using their bodies, which is good, but they're not relating it to something THEY already understand. The motion YOU choose may not mean anything to them. The motion THEY choose may not mean anything to you. But, the key is for each person to use motions that depict the word/phrase by linking it to a thought or memory he or she already possess.

Through emotions.

As a freshman in college, I posted all of Philippians 4:6-7 in my dorm room. I cut each letter out of felt and glued them on the wall, and it took most of the wall. (I'm sure they were happy with me for leaving all that glue on the wall when I moved to a new dorm.) But, I can't think of that verse without going back to that dorm room. Philippians 4:6-7 is tied to an emotion for me.

Through pictures.

We think in pictures…not words. Don't believe me? Close your eyes and have someone say a word. Concentrate on the first thing that comes to your mind. It will be a picture. It won't be the word spelled out in your mind's eye. If the word you are given is "puppy", you'll see a little furry guy of some sort, but you won't see the letters p-u-p-p-y. If the word you are given is "leap", then you'll see someone bounding across a meadow or such, but you won't see the letters l-e-a-p.

Pictures are powerful! So, find ways to connect the Scripture through pictures. Then, when you're trying to move from one section of a Scripture and you're hesitant, the brain will recall the picture and you're back on track. Take photos or find photos in a magazine that remind you of a word or phrase in the Scripture. Depict the Scripture in some art form—Play-Doh®, rebus, comic strip, painting a picture, making stick figures.

Key #3
Understand Unfamiliar Vocabulary

By the age of 6, preschoolers can use at least 2,500 words, but understand almost ten times that many. Through the elementary years, they continue to add to their vocabulary in a range of 6-12 words a day, but these are more abstract and descriptive words. The English language contains about 200,000 words…Wow!

If kids are taking in this much vocabulary, why do we shy away from teaching them unfamiliar words that are found in the Bible? When memorizing Scripture, it is key to have understanding of what it is that you're memorizing. So, you've got to have a grasp of the vocabulary! Vocabulary, and the word development stage, is a key factor in choosing an appropriate version of the Bible to memorize. It needs to both make sense and to stretch the learner just a little.

Once, when I had a group of 75 kids (ages 5 through 5th grade) in front of me for a midweek program, I introduced the key verse of our 8 weeks together. It was Romans 6:23 (NLT), *For the wages of sin is death, but the free gift of God is eternal life through Christ Jesus our Lord.* The moment that the word "wages" came out of my mouth, the thought occurred to me that the kids may not have that word in their vocabularies. So, in my southern Indiana "accent", I asked, "Who knows what wages are?" No one responded.

Again, I asked the question, and it was quite evident that the kids were uncomfortable with me asking, but no one answered. So, I gave them a clue. I said, "This is something your dad may get every week or two." They were now looking at me as if I'd lost my sanity. Then, one little boy, with the boldness to rescue the group, slowly inched his hand up the side of his head. I immediately called on James. His response was, "It's when you get your underwear caught in your crack!" Oh my, the kids thought I was saying "wedgies." They were going to learn this verse as if it said, "the wedgies of sin is death!" My lazy hick accent had thrown them off. When they didn't know what "wages" meant, their brains registered with the next word they could come up with that sounded close and was in their vocabulary. To this day, I have a difficult time reciting Romans 6:23 correctly.

Here are some ways to build the appropriate vocabulary.

- Each child should identify words that are unfamiliar to him/her. Don't worry about others. If they can't pronounce it, they probably don't know it.

- Show kids how to use a dictionary, or put them on the computer to utilize an online dictionary.

- Assign them to highlight three difficult words in the Scripture, even if they think they know them.

- Encourage kids to ask adults what the words mean to them.

- Share in small groups what the new vocabulary words mean.

- Show pictures of any nouns that are new vocabulary (ie., thresh, flax). Use images to cement the meanings into memory.

Key #4
Break Up the Intensity of the Verses with Lots of Activity

Saying the verse over and over and over again isn't the best way to memorize. Did that register with you? I know that's how we've traditionally thought of memorization, but it's just the tip of this iceberg.

First of all, break the Scripture down into phrases so that you group several words together. This way, you're not memorizing 25 individual words, but 5 blocks. There's something about "chunking" the Scripture that makes it more manageable. After all, doing 5 of something feels much easier than doing 25 of it!

Now, for the activity part. I've included all kinds of games in this book that you've probably wondered about. They don't seem to have a lot of connection to the Scripture itself. But wait! There's a method to my madness. Really! When you say whatever it is that you're memorizing over and over, you're hanging out in the exact same spot in your brain. When you do something that causes your brain to move from that spot and take care of something else—take out the garbage, hit a ball into a cup, answer the door, race someone as you balance a book on your head—you force a different part of your brain to function. Then, after completing this little task, your brain has to go on a hunt to find where that Scripture is so you can recall it. That's when it starts moving from short-term memory to long-term memory. When you can locate the verse as you go in and out of activity, you're strengthening the ability to recall it. That's why these games are important. You'll notice that you don't wait to recall the Scripture after the entire game is over, but rather after each round. This gives the kids something fun, and usually physical, to do, and accomplishes lots of opportunities for recall in the midst of it.

Key #5

Share What You Have Learned

The kids have worked hard at memorizing Scripture, but the value isn't in just saying it to themselves. There is great benefit in being able to share it with others.

- It helps the memorizer to internalize the Scripture when he or she can appropriately recall it in a helpful situation.

- Saying it to yourself and saying it to someone else is totally different. The anxiety of recalling it out loud in front of someone else is a hurdle that the memorizer has to overcome to be able to utilize the Scripture in future situations.

- Reciting a Scripture to someone else, and receiving encouragement from that person, is a form of celebration. We don't celebrate enough in the church, so give kids the opportunity to share their Scriptures with anyone and everyone.

Where can kids share and recite?

- Coordinate with the worship leader, and arrange for individuals or groups to recite a Scripture that goes along with the theme of the service.

- Visit adult Sunday school classes to demonstrate what the kids are learning.

- Videotape individual kids saying their verse.

- Give the kids a homework assignment with 10 blanks. They have to get signatures of 10 different people they have said their verse to that week. (It's also a great way to get them comfortable with witnessing.)

Key #6

Choosing the Right Version for You

I can't read the King James Version of the Bible and understand it, much less be able to memorize it to the place where it becomes part of my everyday life. Some people can, but I believe that most of them choose it more out of tradition than out of practical use.

It's God Word—the Bible—Holy Scripture—so none of the versions are WRONG! I believe it's best to memorize out of the version you normally read. The tone is familiar, and when you're reading and you come to a verse you've memorized, it's a moment of encouragement when, without looking, you can say word-for-word what the page says. Now, if you're planning to be a theologian, then maybe there are reasons to choose one version over another because of translation accuracy, but for most of us, it's the daily use that we need to be comfortable with. It needs to fit into our personal culture, style, and personality. It needs to sound like something you would say. This goes for children and adults.

Whichever version you choose, stick with it. Don't memorize some Scriptures from one version and others from another version. It just gets confusing.

Key #7
Stay Motivated

Memorizing Scripture is something you have to keep at. It's a discipline—a holy habit. Many of us have attempted to memorize regularly, but along the way it fell apart. Don't stew over your failures. Look at why you dropped the ball, get up, and start over with a fresh plan.

Remember: Today is always a good day to start memorizing Scripture!

Your failure in the past may have been because of your motivation. Why were you memorizing? Was it …

- For a sticker?

- To win something?

- Because a group was doing it?

- Forced by parents or a teacher?

- So you could boast about what you had accomplished?

If these were the motivation, they're very short-term.

The motivation needs to be that you'll see long-term change in your life.

- To get your mind full of God's truth

- That you desire spiritual maturity

- That you're just downright hungry for God's Word

If you're convinced it's important, you'll be motivated!

And, it really is fun! It's fun to get to know someone, and the Someone you're getting to know is the God of the Universe.

Motivation also comes when you see your progress. Kids (and adults) like to see where they were and where they are now. It's a way of celebrating! Maybe it doesn't feel like a whole lot of motivation when there are only 2 verses memorized, but when you've got a list of 25…oh yeah, you are pushing through and flying high.

In your Bible, highlight each verse you memorize with a special color. Each time you see a green highlight, you know you've committed that one to memory. One day you'll flip through your Bible and it will be glowing with green.

Keep a journal. Each time you memorize a Scripture, write the address (Scripture reference) and the verse in full…of course, by heart. Then, date it.

Find someone to be accountable to. Determine a time when you will say your verses to them. This will also be a guard for any words you may have changed.

Key #8

Incorporate Music

Music is right brain, so it hangs out with long-term memory. Anything you put to music, you're going to remember a lot longer. When you learned your ABCs, more than likely you did so with the use of music. I bet it's difficult for you to say the ABCs without breaking into song. You probably know the words to hundreds of songs. Don't you wish you could say the same thing about the number of verses you have memorized?

So, how can you incorporate music?

- As you say the verse, listen for a rhythm, even if it doesn't appear throughout the entire verse. I have a verse (Ezra 3:11) that I can't wait to get about halfway through so I can break into a rhythm with "Beeecause…the foundation of the house of the Lord was laid."

- There are all kinds of groups that focus on reaching children with the Word of God through song, and their music makes wonderful tools for memorizing Scripture. Seeds Music comes in a variety of styles, and each CD is around a different theme. Want something really edgy, but straight Scripture? Then JumpStart3 is the group for your kids. They will absolutely love this music!

- Put the Scripture to music. Yeah, write your own song. You can use a familiar tune or make one up yourself. Don't be afraid to repeat key words or phrases.

- Create a rap or an echo.

- Use rhythm sticks, a drum, or an oatmeal can to provide a heavy beat.

Key #9

Don't Hurry. Stay Steady.

You know the story of the tortoise and the hare. The two were paired for a race. The hare was obviously much faster, but got sidetracked. The tortoise, though, just kept moving forward at a steady pace and won the race.

Oh, this is so what happens over and over with Scripture memorization. We hurry to memorize a verse, but don't take the time to review and explore it in multiple ways. It ends up wandering around short-term memory for a while, but then gets lost in all the random information stored in the brain.

Too often, we all "study for the test," which is another way to say we procrastinate. If you have an accountability partner, or if the kids are supposed to have a verse memorized for Sunday school, it's highly likely that you wait until just a few minutes before to cram the verse into your brain…but it's going into short-term memory, and that's not where you want it. Going over it a few minutes a day would take the same amount of time, but would guide the Scripture to the part of the brain where it will stay for a long time.

That's why it's so important to determine exactly where and when you'll work on your memorization. Write it down. Tell someone who will keep you accountable. Keep a personal chart. Let's say you decide to concentrate on memorization each day for 15 minutes following dinner. Once you get in the habit of doing that, you'll feel a tug of guilt when you turn on the TV instead. Guilt's a good thing if it gets you back on track! Adults or kids—having a set time and place keeps you moving forward at a steady pace. Keep doing it. You get better with practice. If you stop before the habit is in place, you have to go back to square one and start over.

Once you start experiencing success—like when a verse comes to mind just when you need it, or the pastor starts to quote a Scripture in his sermon and you beat him to it, or you wake up in the middle of the night and a Scripture is on your mind—that's the motivation that you need to keep going at your steady pace.

Slow and steady, reviewing often, stretching and trying to go just a little further each day…that's what moves it into long-term memory and makes you a winner!

Key #10

Eliminate Distractions

- Turn off music, TV, anything that's going to make noise.

- Get away from other people, unless they are helping you memorize.

- Post an indicator that lets others know you are not to be disturbed (like a sign on the door, a shut door, wear a special hat).

- Keep your iPad or a notepad handy, so if you're tempted to think about an errand you need to take care of and you're afraid you'll forget something, jot it down and it's safe. You can then go back to your memorizing.

- Keep anything you need for memorizing together. Maybe you have a ring of Scripture cards, pencil, journal, CD player, and drawing paper that you regularly use. Keep these in a drawer together and not scattered about where you'll be interrupted to go fetch them.

- Set a timer, so you know when your memorizing time is done. You are more likely to focus when you know the clock is ticking.

Key #11

Use "Tricks" to Remember Numbers

One of the most difficult parts about memorizing Scripture is remembering the numbers. So, there are a few approaches you can take to this.

Identify a picture that goes along with each number, 1-10. Then, associate those objects with your Scripture address. Here are some examples, but make your own associations.

- 1 – foam victory finger, #1
- 2 – twins
- 3 – blind mice
- 4 – seasons
- 5 – gold rings (from the "12 Days of Christmas")
- 6 – dice
- 7 – days in the week
- 8 – box of crayons
- 9 – cat (has 9 lives)
- 10 – fingers

Associate weird things with the number:

- Micah 6:8 – I think that Micah was tall, probably 6'8"

- Esther 4:14 – I associate with the 4/14 window in ministry to kids.

- Job 19:25 – 1925 was a BAD year (I don't know if it really was, but that's what stuck with me.)

Key #12
Utilize All the Multiple Intelligences

Each person has 8 different ways they take in information. These are called the Multiple Intelligences or "Smarts." Individuals vary, though, in how strong they are in these different smarts. They prefer some and struggle with others. The beautiful thing about Multiple Intelligences is that through exposure and exercise, you can actually strengthen a weak smart. This is incredible news, because when a learner has substantial strength in all areas, it doesn't matter how information is presented, he/she is comfortable in taking it in.

If you always present Scripture memorization in words, then the person who has a low word smart is going to struggle constantly. That's why we have to experience the Scripture that we're memorizing in a variety of ways, utilizing as many Multiple Intelligences as possible. You want to come at the Scripture from different angles.

The Multiple Intelligences are listed here with an example of an exercise that could be used from that smart.

- Word smart – vocabulary studies and using word grids

- Math smart – putting phrases from the verse in order, using card rings

- Music smart – put the Scripture to music or rhythm

- People smart – say the Scripture to many different people

- Self smart – set aside a time to be alone and work on the Scripture by yourself, daydream about how this verse could come up in conversation

- Body smart – create motions or a dance, play a game that will cause you to search your brain to recall the Scripture

- Picture smart – paint a picture about your Scripture, create a rebus

- Nature smart – find a relaxing scenic spot to memorize

Key #13

Identify Triggers

The more you PLAY WITH and explore the Scripture, the more inroads and triggers you have to assist your long-term memory in recalling it. What are triggers? They are special, vital tools in your toolbox for Scripture memorization. They help you move from one chunk to the next. They are the prompts that help you get started.

You may have a verse memorized, but it's so difficult to get started—to remember that first word. I'm sure you've done this before: Someone says the first phrase in a Scripture and you finish it…but, there was no way you were going to be able to start it on your own from the very beginning. This is one of the most important places to focus your attention in memorizing—to come up with something that will trigger that first word in your memory. Just saying the verse over and over is the long, more difficult way. Pause a few moments and figure out an association—a trigger—that will connect with that particular verse.

Take a moment as you begin to memorize a verse and figure out the launching trigger.

You can also use triggers as reminders to review your verse. It may be something you do periodically throughout the day, something you hear, or something you notice. Some examples of a trigger that reminds you to practice are:

- Every time you hear the church bells chime, you say your verse.

- Every time you open the refrigerator door.

- Every time you get a text.

- Every time you open a book.

- Every time you put your clothes in the hamper.

Key #14

The 4 Rs: Repeat, Relate, Recall, Review

Repeat. When you first start with a verse, you need to say it over and over. That's usually where teachers stop when working on Scripture memorization with their students. They use a diehard technique of writing the verse on the board and erasing one word at a time until the verse disappeared and the kids can recite the verse without thinking. They've managed to install it in short-term memory, but more than likely it's gone by the time the child reaches the car. Repeating is only the first step. Repeating the verse gives you a sense of the rhythm, alerts you to key words, and helps you plan your strategy of attack on memorizing.

Relate. Explore the verse until you know what it is communicating. Read the verses before and after. Learn about the theme of the book where the verse is found. Add new words to your personal vocabulary. Draw it. Talk to others about what the verse means to them. Dig in and get to know the verse.

Recall. I've included a whole section of random games you can play with kids that will exercise their ability to recall. You may think the games have nothing to do with memorizing, but they're interrupting the thought process, so the memorizer has to search his brain to recall the verse. It's like strengthening a muscle. When you have to find the verse in your brain again—you need to recall it—which means you have to find the picture you drew, or recall the trigger word that gets you started, or relate the theme of the book to the verse you're searching for. Interruptions—playing one short round of a game—greatly strengthen the ability to recall, which therefore moves the memorization into long-term memory. **It is much more important to recall than to repeat.** Okay, read that again. Being able to pull up a verse in the middle of a totally different activity is more important than saying it 10 times, one after another. **You memorize when you practice recalling, not when you repeat.** This is preparation for those times when you're in the middle of a conversation and want to share a verse. That's the ultimate recall! At the beginning, it's important to repeat the verse until it's at least partially contained in short-term memory, because if it's not, then there's nothing to recall.

**If you want to memorize Scripture,
practice RECALLING, not repeating!**

Review. You'll never keep Scripture memorized if you don't review it. It's important that you provide games and opportunities for kids to go over verses they learned previously. Review can get quite time-consuming once you've got a great number of verses memorized. They will fade from your memory, though, if you don't set aside a time—maybe once every 6 weeks—to go through them. Personally, I use one of my memorization time periods each week for review and during that time I don't try to learn anything new. (My long-term memory needs lots of assistance!)

Notes:

_____

_____

_____

_____

_____

Methods of Memorization

In simplest of terms, memorizing is finding a way to code something into your brain. The process of connecting with that code can take place in a lot of different ways. Some methods of memorizing will not resonate with you, and they don't seem to do any good. But others…and every learner will have a repertoire…will be the sweet spot for memorizing. The best method for memorizing is the one that the individual person figures out. That may be one, but more than likely, it will be a combination of several.

Don't be afraid to try some new methods, especially if your method of memorizing Scripture has been the erase-a-word and say it again…erase-a-word and say it again … erase-a-word and say it again…yawn…zzzzzz.

Method #1

Chunking

Chunking is a way of organizing large pieces of information. It's overwhelming to look at a long passage and try to dive into the entire thing. Instead, break it down into chunks that make sense. This can be sentences, phrases, or parts that have a rhythm to them. The more you master the art of chunking, the greater the amount of information you can memorize. How cool is that!

When I memorized Isaiah 53:11 (ESV), here's how I divided it into chunks:

Chunk #1: *Out of the anguish of his soul he shall see and be satisfied;* – When I first read this, I felt a rhythm, and so I always say this part with a beat…a metronome clicking away inside me.

Chunk #2: *by his knowledge shall the righteous one, my servant,* – I see a mental picture of a head (knowledge) and then 2 names for the same one (righteous one and my servant).

Chunk #3: *make many to be accounted righteous,* – This sounds so authoritative to me the way it's worded, so I chunk this one in a voice that sounds almost as if giving orders.

Chunk #4: *and he shall bear their iniquities.* – This is a phrase that I relate to the book of Isaiah, especially the word "iniquities." So, mentally, I thought, "Wrap this verse up with a theme of Isaiah."

Here's another way to utilize chunking and your music smart. Divide a Scripture into chunks and then add a rhythm response by inserting some claps and/or stomps.

> In the beginning (clap, clap, clap),
>
> God created (clap, clap, clap)
>
> the heavens and the earth (clap, clap, clap),
>
> the heavens and the earth (clap, clap, clap).
>
> (Genesis 1:1, NASB)
>
> Trust in the LORD (stomp, stomp, clap)
>
> with all your heart (stomp, stomp, clap)
>
> And do not lean (stomp, stomp, clap)
>
> on your own understanding. (stomp, stomp, clap)
>
> In all your ways (stomp, stomp, clap)
>
> acknowledge Him (stomp, stomp, clap)
>
> And He will make (stomp, stomp, clap)
>
> your paths straight (stomp, stomp, clap).
>
> (Proverbs 3:5-6, NASB)

When you utilize chunking, each piece has it's own trigger—something that gives you clues as to how the pieces fit together. If you'll take the time to break the verse or passage down, you'll memorize faster and easier…much easier than saying it over and over again until your brain just wants to throw up its little gray matter hands in surrender.

Method #2

The Power of Pictures

Just this morning, I once again proved the power of pictures when memorizing Scripture. The verse I was working on was Amos 5:24 (ESV), *But let justice roll down like waters, and righteousness like an ever-flowing stream*. It just wasn't clicking. I wasn't getting anywhere, and it's such a short verse. So, I started through different methods that might facilitate making a connection. Pictures! This verse is full of imagery—pictures. So, I sketched out a picture, and refined it as I spoke the verse several more times.

Amos 5:24

JUSTICE

RIGHTEOUSNESS

I'm not an artist, and that's quite evident. You don't have to be. Use stick figures to draw a picture that gives you a point of reference. As soon as the picture was developed, I knew the verse. Incredible! It really is fun to put these in a notebook and start a collection.

For kids and adults, sitting down to draw out a verse is extremely helpful and meaningful. It's time-consuming, but it moves the memorization process along at a rapid pace, so it's worth it— really worth it!

A camera is a powerful tool for creating pictures. Put a camera in the hands of your kids—after all, most of them have access to a cell phone—so they can create still photos that depict the verse. These can be photos of individual objects, or they can put together several items. Example: if they are memorizing Genesis 1:26 (NASB), *Let Us make man in Our image, according to Our likeness,* then the picture could be of a man they made out of Legos® or by putting pieces of fruit and cheese together. As that verse goes on, it describes all that man is to rule over, so the photo taken could be of a menagerie of stuffed animals, figurines of animals, and maybe even their dog lying in the midst of them. Do you see how through pictures, you can make a verse your own and connect with it on a personal level?

Keep it interesting by incorporating pictures in a variety of ways.

- Use different mediums to paint with: water colors, powdered sugar paint, chalk, finger paints, pudding, markers, crayons, colored pencils, dry erase markers, fabric paints, charcoal

- Use different utensils to paint with: toothbrush, sponge, marshmallow, Bingo marker, bath puff, communion cup, flyswatter, fork, feather

- Play dough

- Wet sand

Method #3

Sing It

Even if you're not musical, you can put Scripture to familiar tunes. You don't have to write a new tune or record the latest hit. Pick a tune that you have grown up with—one that is second nature—and see if the verse will fit. You may have to try several tunes, but on many verses, you'll find some nice notes and rhythm to go with the verse. You may not be able to do it with the entire passage, but choose a chunk. Or, to make it fit into the tune better, repeat a prominent phrase.

Anytime you put something to music…remember, you are moving it into long-term memory. It may sound a little silly to be doing this, but take the attitude that you are praising God in song by singing His Word back to Him.

Here are some tunes to try:

- "Jesu, Joy of Man's Desiring"

- "Three Blind Mice"

- "Amazing Grace"

- "Hey Jude"

- "The Farmer in the Dell"

- "I'll Fly Away"

- "ABC Song"

- "Can't Help Falling in Love with You"

Method #4

Use a Scripture Organization Guide

Use an organization guide for a group of verses that you are attempting to memorize because of something they have in common. Some common ways to organize groups of Scripture are:

- Memorize a key verse from each book of the Bible that speaks to that book's theme.

- Memorize a verse that begins with each letter of the alphabet. (There's a great resource for a free set of alphabet Scriptures at icanteachmychild.com.)

- Memorize topical verses that go along with a particular study you're doing. If kids are using a 6-week special curriculum about prayer, then choose verses for them to work on during that time that specifically address prayer.

The great thing about the organization guides is that something about one Scripture acts as a trigger for the next one. You're learning them in an order, and you'll create your own associations. This is one of my personal favorites.

Method #5

Letter Grid

Give each child a blank grid made up of ¾" squares that fill a sheet of paper. In the upper left corner they will write the first letter of the first word in their passage. In the box to the right of that one, just like they were reading a sentence, write the first letter of the second word. Continue writing the first letter of each word in the entire passage, putting a space between the sentences. In a very short amount of time, the child will be able to read the entire passage by using first letter prompters as an aid.

Studies have shown that if we see the first and last letter of a word, it doesn't matter what order the letters in between are. We'll still be able to read the words. This method operates on that same concept, except the child is identifying the word with only one of those cues.

There's a helpful tool on a website that will take your text and convert it to the first letter of each word for you. It even keeps words in the proper lower or upper case. Then, you can print it out. It'll save you a lot of time, so give it a try. http://www.productivity501.com/how-to-memorize-verbatim-text/

Method #6

Identify a List

Is there a list in the verse? Are you scratching your head and wondering what that means? Look at the verse and see if there are three or more things, people, or characteristics listed. Identifying the list gives you a chunk to work on rather than tackling the verse in its entirety. In other words, it breaks it down into pieces. Galatians 5:22-23 is a perfect example where the fruit of the Spirit is listed: love, joy, peace, patience, kindness, goodness, faithfulness, gentleness, and self-control.

Look at 1 Chronicles 29:11 (ESV): *"Yours, O LORD, is the greatness, and the power, and the glory, and the victory, and the majesty, for all that is in the heavens and in the earth is yours. Yours is the kingdom, O LORD, and you are exalted as head above all."*

Can you identify the list in this verse? Micah 6:8 (ESV), *"He has told you, O man, what is good; and what does the LORD require of you but to do justice, and to love kindness, and to walk humbly with your God?"*

When you identify a list and memorize it separately, you build around it. You may struggle to get the few words before, but then when you get to that chunk of a list, you whiz right through it…and that feels good!

Method #7

Enter It

Type it (for those of you who are used to typewriter lingo), but for everyone else in the computer age, ENTER IT in your computer. Especially if you are a proficient typist, this can be quite beneficial. Hitting the keys and putting together the words one-by-one, slows down the Scripture in your mind. It doesn't just fall out of your mouth. You have to wait on each word to be completely entered before you can move on. It frequently causes you to start in the middle of the Scripture and pick up where your typing stopped. Writing it out longhand also falls under this method.

Find different places to enter it: iPad®, cell phone, screen saver, recipe card, Post-It® note, bookmark, or a to-do list.

Notes:

No More Excuses!

Even though you understand the importance and have learned some keys to memorization, you may still find yourself waffling on whether or not to commit to the task. Maybe you're not sure your brain is up to the challenge and you fear failure. Maybe you even think God will be disappointed if you try to memorize His Word and can't do it or just give up. I want to encourage you that the only way you are going to fail at Scripture memorization is not to try! You can do this—one Bible verse at a time. Let's take a look at two common excuses and get them out of the way, so you can move forward to success!

Excuse #1

I Just Don't Have Time

Really? Is that what you really think? Is that your excuse for not memorizing Scripture? Sorry, I'm not buying what you're trying to sell me. We all have time, or we make time, for the things that are important to us. When you decide that memorizing God's Word is of super high value to you, then let me help you see how you can make this excuse—and the truth you perceive it to have—go away.

We're all busy, and it seems like the only solution is to have more hours in the day. (The only one I know who actually received that gift was Joshua when God made the sun and moon stand still…but don't hold your breath…I've tried asking.) But, if we had more hours, we'd just fill it with more stuff, and we'd wish we had even more hours. What God asks of us, though, is to make the most of what He has given us, and that includes our time. Remember the guys who were given the talents? God wasn't upset with the amount of return any of them got, except for the one who buried his—the one who refused to even look for a way to make his investment multiply.

Time management. That's what I want to talk to you about for a few minutes. I'm not going to give you a way to schedule your day, but I would like to get you thinking about where YOU could reclaim lost time in your day—time that you don't even realize you have. All you're looking for is 5-10 minutes each day.

Adults and kids alike have time they can reclaim.

Reclaim the time while you are going through your morning routine. Instead of letting my head just rest in some dead space, I can actually get my brain functioning at full blast by energizing it with Scripture memorization while wielding a curling iron.

Use commercial time during one half-hour program. A typical 30-minute program is actually only 22 minutes long. That leaves you 8 minutes. Perfect! Each time a commercial comes on, push the mute button and stay put. You can get that snack some other time.

This is actually an excellent way to memorize because you are breaking up the activity. After each segment of the show, your brain has to recall what you had previously worked on, and that makes it much stronger. (And without the trips to the fridge, you may even lose a pound or two.)

Multitask during jogging, walking, working out, or using the treadmill. Instead of putting in your earplugs and piping in music, put in the earplugs and recall OUT LOUD the Scriptures you have memorized and the one you're working on.

Drive time. It may be that you have a daily commute, but even if you don't, most people have a time during the day when they have to run at least one errand—round trip 5-10 minutes. We all sing in the car or talk back at the radio (you know you do); then, it's a small step to use that time to say Scriptures OUT LOUD while you're driving. Get the kids to review their Scriptures on the way to school or when they're waiting for the bus.

Add it to a daily routine. Kids can help set the table. Encourage them to put all the spoons in place while saying one verse—the "spoon verse." Then, they can say a different verse as they put the forks in place, another for the plates, and another for the glasses, etc.

Trouble sleeping? Up in the middle of the night with thoughts of everything you have to do tomorrow on your mind? Start reviewing your Scriptures and you'll be back to sleep in a jiffy…not that it bores you to sleep…but it gets your mind on something that's not so stressful.

Boys who play basketball and shoot 200 baskets a day in the driveway by themselves can reclaim that time and work on Scripture memorization while zipping the net. So, what rehearsal or repetition do your kids do to get better at a skill? Can they include working on Scripture memorization while doing that?

Are you in the habit of hitting the snooze button 3 times before actually getting out of bed? There's an extra 20 minutes if you'll just get up on the first ring. Oh, come on, you can do this!

Okay, it's time for you to take a good look at your day. Where are the holes when you're not really engaged in anything? What activities do you do without thought that you could reclaim for Scripture memorization? Don't move on until you've decided on a specific time you will personally reclaim.

Instead of _____ **(watching TV?),**

playing _____ **(video games),**

I will use that time to memorize Scripture.

Excuse #2

Memorizing Is Difficult for Me...I'm Old!

When you're young and in school, in addition to learning going on in the course of experiences, studying is part of your daily routine. But, we get out of the habit of delving into a new area and absorbing what we can. It's like when you've been exercising regularly and you step away from it. The more time that passes, the harder it is, and the longer it takes, to get those muscles strengthened. That does not mean that you can't, though! You are never too old to start learning something new. You are never too old to start memorizing Scripture!

Memorizing Scripture MAKES YOU YOUNGER. Oh, I got your attention! It doesn't take the wrinkles away, but it is great for the gray matter between your ears. Memorization is one of the best exercises for increasing the neuroplasticity of your brain. Just like walking is good for your muscles and brain, memorizing helps strengthen the connections in your brain. One of the common complaints as you get older is that you're forgetting things. That's because the connections aren't strong anymore. Memorize and you'll help that.

Your brain has the amazing capacity to change. It can make new connections, adapt, and react in new ways if the right stimulation is present. That's where the Multiple Intelligences come in—8 ways that we all take in information. (See more about this under Key to Memorization #12.) The Multiple Intelligences help you create the right environment for you as you memorize.

Two other important influencers in your ability to memorize are rest and exercise. When you get the proper amount of sleep, your brain is ready to work on memorization. While you are asleep, your brain "takes out the garbage." It gets rid of the clutter and gives you a fresh start. That's one reason I do my memorization early in the morning. It's when my brain is functioning at its peak. Another benefit to a good night's rest is that your memories are consolidated when you are in your deepest stage of sleep. Rest isn't just essential when you begin to memorize verses, but it's a way to get those Scriptures to move into long-term memory.

The other influencer is exercise. When you walk, your brain also exercises. It constantly moves from giving the command for your left foot, and then a different place gives the command for your right foot...back and forth in the brain...strengthening connections. Exercise also increases the oxygen flow to the brain, and we all know that when you can breathe, you feel better. Years ago my husband had a serious head injury from a fall. As soon as he was home and able, the doctors emphasized that it was critical that he walk. Why? His brain needed the exercise. So, get plenty of rest and exercise—two things that will help you memorize and keep you feeling younger.

Several years ago I presented a workshop in a Mississippi community. In my workshops, I always recommend *Egermeier's® Bible Story Book* as a resource for teachers and parents. A year or so later, I was asked to return to that same place to do another set of

training sessions. As people were arriving, the host pointed out an elderly (90+-year-old) woman sitting at a table. She encouraged me to go to the woman and ask her about her *Egermeier's* experience, so I did. The woman held her *Egermeier's* lovingly as she showed me the bookmark about two-thirds of the way through. Then she said, "I've been in church all my life, but I've never been able to read the Bible. I used this *Egermeier's* to teach myself how to read, and since I got this from you the last time you were here, I'm this far. For the first time in my life, I understand the Bible stories and can read them for myself." If she can learn how to read at the age of 90+…if she can learn something new, something as phenomenal as reading…then I know you can learn how to memorize Scripture.

Notes:

_____

_____

_____

_____

_____

_____

_____

_____

_____

_____

_____

_____

_____

_____

_____

Notes:

Notes:

Explore the Meaning

Even though a child may think they understand the meaning of a verse, everyone who has ever spent any time in Scripture knows that you never understand to the fullest. There's always another aspect…or another thought…or another aha moment.

Memorizing is much easier if you have a base understanding of the passage. Each learner, though, must search for understanding in a variety of ways. Explore the verse from different angles. The objective is to get comfortable with each word in the verse and connect with it. Let's look at some activities that will help promote understanding.

ASK QUESTIONS

Challenge kids to write down the answers to 3 questions about the Scripture. Here are some samples that will help you direct them.

- Who is talking?
- What does a certain phrase mean? (such as, "passes understanding")
- How does this verse fit into the theme of this book of the Bible?
- What does a prominent word in the verse mean? ("glory")
- Why is this verse important to be included in the Bible?
- Have you ever felt this way?
- What part of the verse stands out to you?

In group time, discuss the answers the kids came up with.

PHOTOGRAPHS

Arm kids with a cell phone so they can use the camera. As they think about the Scripture, encourage them to take a picture that depicts a word or phrase in the Scripture. These pictures can be of something they randomly capture, or they can be posed shots. If you wanted to take a picture of the phrase "have mercy on me," what would it look like?

BEFORE AND AFTER

Read the verses before and after the one you are memorizing, so you can understand its context. Memorizing a stand-alone verse, you could easily interpret the verse incorrectly. Knowing what leads up to the verse and what follows it lends to a more complete understanding.

MAKE REFERENCE

As you teach, bring the Scripture the kids (or you) are memorizing into the lesson. Refer to it often. Each time you refer to it, you're providing an additional connection point of understanding. So, use the verse in appropriate contexts as much as possible.

INTERVIEW

One of the best ways to grasp understanding of a verse is to interview people about their take on it. What does this verse mean to you? Choose people you admire because of their devotion to God's Word. Make sure you write down the main thing that was said and the person's name. This is a great thing to include in a Scripture memorization journal! The other benefit to interviewing is that kids connect with mentors who will be valuable for years in their faith development…maybe even for a lifetime.

PARAPHRASE

Write the verse/passage in your own words. Emphasize that the kids do not have to stick with the same words used in Scripture. Paraphrasing is basically answering the question: When I read this, what does it say to me?

PLAY-DOH® ART

Needed:

- supply of Play-Doh®
- waxed paper

Give each child a supply of Play-Doh®. It doesn't matter that it is the correct color for what they want to do; in fact, giving them one color to work with doesn't seem to stifle their creativity at all.

Encourage them to think about the verse and then use the Play-Doh® to create a way of telling others something about that verse. Don't give too many instructions so that their minds are free to go any direction they want.

Provide a time for the children to display their creations and explain the connection that they made.

The following is a recipe for homemade Play-Doh®. There are also a wide variety of Play-Doh® recipes online.

Homemade Play-Doh® Recipe

- 1½ c. flour
- ¾ c. salt
- 3 T. oil
- 1½ t. cream of tartar
- 1½ c. water
- food coloring
- waxed paper
- nonstick 2-qt. saucepan
- airtight container

Add the food coloring to the water. Mix all the dry ingredients together in the nonstick saucepan. Then, add the colored water and stir until everything is moist. Heat the mixture over a low heat, constantly stirring. It will appear very lumpy, but just keep stirring. When it goes to one large ball and pulls away from the sides of the pan, put it out on a piece of waxed paper and knead. Oh, by the way, the lumps have mysteriously disappeared. Enjoy the nice warm dough on your hands…oooh, that feels good! Store in an airtight container, and this Play-Doh® will stay good for a very long time.

MAGAZINE REBUS

Needed:

- glue stick
- large piece of plain paper
- marker
- old magazines
- scissors

The object of this exercise is to replace as many words in the Scripture to be memorized with pictures or the actual words found in magazines. Cut the pictures and words out and assemble them to create a rebus. Glue each piece in place on the large piece of paper so that the verse can be interpreted and read by the additions from the magazine. If some words cannot be found, then the children can write those in themselves or draw a picture that depicts that word. Give the children an opportunity to share their creations with the rest of the group.

The children have to look at each word individually, and explore how it could be portrayed through picture or creative lettering. In this concentrated effort to look at each word, those words and pictures are transferred to mental pictures that will help children remember. The magazine pieces act as mental prompts and cues.

MAKE A REBUS

Each child will create a rebus. The kids will put the verse on their paper, but substitute pictures for words as often as they can. It is not necessary that the pictures be of the actual word. The pictures may depict sounds or syllables, rather than the full word. (Examples: "seen" could be a set of eyes. "Heard" might be an ear. "Who" could be an owl. "Him" could be pointing at the edge of a skirt.) Don't tell the kids what to draw; just let them connect their own pictures to the words.

RANDOM Games and Activities

Utilizing a variety of games and activities makes Scripture memorization interesting, engaging, and fun for kids. These are suggested for your use and to also spur you to use your own creativity in crafting ways for your kids to work toward hiding God's Word in their hearts and minds.

AUDIO RECORDINGS

Needed:

- voice recorder on a cell phone

Option #1

Allow a child time to read through the Scripture out loud until he is comfortable with all the words, punctuation, and their inflection. You don't want him to struggle at any point.

On a cell phone that they have access to daily, record them saying the Scripture using an app like Voice Recorder. This becomes a good tool to use when they are working on memorization on their own. They can turn on the recording and practice along with someone…them! This is especially beneficial for your auditory learners.

Option #2

You can't be there all the time when kids are working on their memorization, but you can be an encouragement through audio recordings. Record a phrase and then leave enough time blank for the child to repeat what you've said. Record the next phrase and leave a response blank. Continue doing this until you've completed the verse. Then say, "Now, let's try the whole thing together." Slowly, recite the entire verse so the child can say it along with you.

This is similar to when a child is learning to write. We give them letters that are made out of dotted lines. They trace over the dotted lines, filling in the blanks in between. Once they've done that enough times, they're ready to write several letters next to one another.

BACK AND FORTH

Needed:

- bell
- masking tape

Put down some 2-foot masking tape lines or lay down some yardsticks. Do as many of these as you have room for. Only one child can play at each tape line or yardstick.

Option #1:

The kids will stand with their feet together on one side of the line. At the signal, they will start hopping back and forth across their line, with feet together, as fast as they can. When the bell rings, then everyone stops on one side of their line. Choose RIGHT or LEFT. All the kids who stopped on that side of their line will say the verse together.

Option #2:

Each child will stand with feet together on one side of the line. They will hop back and forth across the line, keeping their feet together as they do, and saying one word of the verse with each hop.

Add this activity to your Mosey In time, because the children can do this on their own as everyone arrives. When you utilize that time while you're waiting for everyone to mosey in, you're reclaiming it to pour the Word of God into kids.

CAN YOU DO IT?

Needed:

- bold dark marker
- duct tape
- empty aluminum cans
- stopwatch
- strips of white paper
- tape

Prepare some empty aluminum cans for play by hammering down any sharp edges and then covering the open edge with duct tape. Count the number of words in the verse you are memorizing. Make a can for each of those words by wrapping a piece of white paper around the can with the word written on it in bold dark letters. Put the cans in a box or bag that is labeled with the Scripture reference. To start, the leader will say, "CAN you do it?" The player will then empty the contents of the bag and try to put the cans in order as quickly as possible so that it says the Scripture being memorized. When the verse is completed, the player raises his hands in the air and says, "Yes, I can!" Players can keep track of their own times on each verse and compete against themselves, trying to improve their times each week.

Option #1:

Each time the children work on a new verse, prepare another sack of cans, labeled with that Scripture reference. The children can time themselves as they dump out one sack of cans, put it together, and then put it back in the sack. They can then move to the next bag to put together another verse. Times can be kept for each individual verse or an overall time of how long it took for all the verses to be put together. Use different color paper for each verse to help identify when they have moved to the next verse and for easy sorting if the cans from different verses get combined.

Option #2:

Instead of white paper, use wrapping paper for the Christmas season or colors that represent a certain holiday or time of the year.

CLAP REPLACEMENT

Say the entire verse together. Then, ask one of the children to choose one of the words from the verse that he wants to eliminate. Say the verse together again, only this time when you come to the word that has been eliminated, everyone will clap instead of saying the word. Mentally, the children will be saying the word, but only the clap will indicate where it is supposed to be.

CREATIVE MOVEMENT

Go word-by-word or phrase-by-phrase through the Scripture. The children will relate the word or phrase to a motion they can create with their bodies. In this exercise, each word or phrase has something physical that it is identified with. It is very important that the children come up with these motions **on their own** and that the leader doesn't hand them a set of motions to do. The leader, though, should be ready to add some options or encourage a different path of thinking when the children get stuck. The entire group can work on motions that they all agree on and can do in unison, or each child can create his personal motions that he more specifically identifies with.

CROSSWORD PUZZLES

Needed:

- paper
- pencil

The kids are not doing a crossword puzzle, but creating their own. By putting it together themselves, they get comfortable with the words, and it's a much better learning experience than filling in blanks for what someone else has worked through.

Challenge the kids to put a crossword puzzle together using as many of the key words in their Scripture as possible. There's no need to write out the clues. Just link the words together.

Once they have their puzzle together, then the challenge is to say the verse, pointing to the key words in the puzzle as they go. It's not as easy as it sounds!

SCRABBLE® CROSSWORD PUZZLES

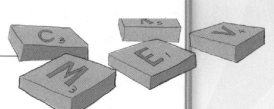

Needed:

- lots of Scrabble® tiles

Create a crossword puzzle with key words from the verse, just like above. This time, though, instead of using paper and pencil, use Scrabble® tiles. The kids can work individually or as a group, adding words to the puzzle whenever they have the letters to make up the word and a place to attach it.

LOLLIPOP WORDS

Needed:

- glue
- marker
- poster board
- scissors
- tongue depressors

Make a 4" diameter poster board circle for each word in the memory verse. Write one word from the verse on each circle in large letters. Then, glue each circle to a tongue depressor. Give each child two of the tongue depressors. Now, practice the verse. The person with the first word of the verse will hold up their tongue depressor. Then, the person with the second word will hold up theirs. Don't put them down. See how fast you can go through all the words.

MOVE IT AROUND

Needed:

- drinking straws
- pieces of lightweight paper

Write each word phrase from the Scripture you are memorizing on a slip of paper. During a certain season or holiday, you can put the word phrases on special cut-outs representing that time of year. For example: snowflakes, leaves, pumpkins, flowers, Christmas tree, piece of fruit. Continue writing the phrases on individual papers until the entire Scripture passage is done, along with the reference. You can make sets for individuals, teams, or for family members.

Give each person a drinking straw. Each group will get a set of papers that are turned upside down on a table. Mix them up. When someone gives the signal, everyone will turn the "leaves" over and put the word phrases in order to form the Scripture being memorized. However, once the papers are turned over, the participants are only allowed to move them by sucking on their straws to pick them up.

ALTERNATE VERSION

Needed:

- cookie sheet
- magnet
- paper clips
- pieces of lightweight paper

You can do the same thing but put a paper clip on each piece of paper. Lay all the pieces of paper with word phrases on them on a cookie sheet. Using a magnet underneath the cookie sheet, move the pieces around until the Scripture passage is in the correct order.

OBJECT LESSON

Needed:

- 6 objects

Look at the Scripture closely and see what objects you associate with certain words. Now, actually find at least 6 of those objects. Lay the objects in a pile or in random order where everyone can see.

As the kids recite the Scripture, pick up the appropriate object. The object becomes the trigger that takes you to the next phrase. It's a picture that you'll have in mind, even after the objects are no longer present.

As a review, you can display the objects and have the kids pick up the correct associative object as they recite the verse.

PUZZLES

Needed:

- old 24-piece children's puzzles

- permanent marker

- wide dark marker

- zip-lock bag

Obtain some old children's puzzles that have no more than 24 pieces. Put the puzzle together and then flip it over so the plain brown side is showing. Write the memory verse in large letters on the backside of the puzzle with a dark marker. Try to keep the entire word on a piece, unless it is a very long word. Take the puzzle apart and place the pieces in a zip-lock bag labeled with the Scripture reference.

The kids will take the pieces out of the bag and try to put the puzzle together, upside down. This works best if the children have their own puzzles or if they work in pairs. It's also a great activity to incorporate during that time when you're waiting for everyone to arrive. If you are using this to review verses that have been previously memorized, each bag could contain a different verse. When the child completes one puzzle, they can trade bags and work on a different verse.

ROCKY ROAD

Needed:

- fine point black markers
- sandwich bags
- smooth rocks

Give the kids access to smooth rocks. (You can get bags of these at a dollar store near the candles. There's enough for about 6-8 kids in each bag. Or try a landscape supplier.)

Using a fine-point permanent black marker, the kids will write each word of the verse on a single rock until they have the entire verse written out on their set of rocks. Make sure they include the reference on one or two rocks. Then, they should put their rocks back in their bag. Shake up the bag and challenge them to put the verse in order.

Send the bag of rocks home with the kids so they can practice later and show their parents.

SCRIPTURE DOMINOES

Needed:

- black construction paper
- sandwich bags
- white marker

Use a paper cutter to make lots of dominoes 2" x 4" out of black construction paper. Go though all of them and draw a white line at the halfway point, to mimic how a domino is divided. Write the words from the Scripture in order, one word at one end of the domino and the next word at the other end of the domino. Make sure you turn the dominoes different directions as you continue writing the words of the rest of the Scripture on them. This will make for an interesting domino pattern as the kids work with them, rather than them make a long domino train.

Put all the dominoes for one Scripture, along with a domino that has the Scripture address on it, in a sandwich bag. The kids will put the dominoes together by matching dominoes with the next word, whether they are going vertically or horizontally.

Keep these sets, because they are great for review and for "Mosey In" time, as kids arrive… moseying in.

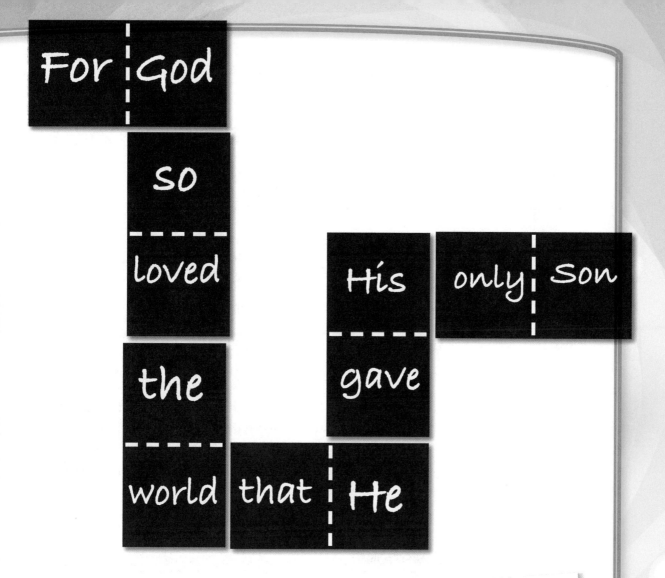

SCRIPTURE JOURNAL

Needed:

- notebook

- paper

- pencil

College composition books are good for this exercise, and they're really, really cheap when school supplies go on sale in late summer.

Scripture journals are great for kids and adults alike. At the top of the page, the journalist will write the Scripture address. Below that, they will write out the entire passage, long hand, and the version that it comes from. Every page will have these 2 elements. From there, though, the pages will be quite different.

In this journal, you want to record anything you've used as an aid to your memorization of that passage.

So, draw your little stick figures that become a picture tool for you.

You could include a rebus.

Write out what the verse means to you.

Include definitions of any words you weren't familiar with.

Write out what other people shared with you about the meaning of this verse.

You also want to include personal things about the verse.

When did you find it particularly useful in everyday life?

When did you hear it mentioned in a sermon or study?

Have you been able to pray this verse? Describe the situation.

You want to leave plenty of blank space following each Scripture entry, because at different times—a week later, a year later, or years down the road—you can add to it. You'll want to include aha moments when this verse came to mean something new to you, when God revealed more about what He wanted to say through His written Word. You are not necessarily done with a page when you've completed the memorization.

SCULPTING BALLOON MOTIONS

Needed:

- balloon pump
- sculpting balloons

Give each child an inflated sculpting balloon. Do not fool yourself into thinking you can blow these balloons up the traditional way. No…you need a balloon pump. They're usually about $4.00 and can be purchased where balloons are sold.

The kids will use the sculpting balloons to create motions for the Scripture, rather than using traditional motions with their arms and hands.

SIGN LANGUAGE

Needed:

- book of sign language

This activity is different from creative movement in that the children are given specific motions that are universally identified with words in a specific sign language. Some of the motions are easily identified with the word or concept and you can see the relationship. Other motions in sign language do not have an obvious connection to the word or concept.

There are books of sign language, such as *The Joy of Signing* or an *ASL Dictionary*, that you can refer to for help in getting correct form. If you know someone who is well versed in sign language, it would be delightful to have them teach the verse to the children. This could even become a regular monthly visitor that the children look forward to being with and learning from.

STADIUM CHANT

Warm up the children by getting them comfortable with the stadium rhythm of "stomp-stomp-clap, stomp-stomp-clap" (that you hear to the "We Will Rock You" cheer). Now that they are almost doing the rhythm without thinking, they will continue the rhythm while saying the Scripture reference and the verse. Sometimes two words will go on one stomp, and other times syllables of a word may be spread over several beats. You're tapping into your music intelligence with this beat, which moves the memorization into long-term memory much quicker. Enjoy!

TENT CARD RELAY

Needed:

- masking tape

- spring clothespins

- supply of tent cards

This game is done best in a large room or outside. Write the memory verse on tent cards, putting one word on each card. (A tent card is when you fold a piece of card stock or poster board so that it will stand, in a tent shape.) Each team needs its own set of tent cards. Scramble the cards and set them out where they can be read at the other end of the room. Apply a strip of masking tape on the floor, in a completely different area, to designate where the cards will be placed as they are put in order. Give each team a spring clothespin.

When the relay begins, the first team member takes the team spring clothespin and runs down to the tent cards. He or she chooses the first word of the verse and picks it up only using the clothespin. That player then runs to their designated place on the masking tape line and sets the tent card at one end of the line. That player returns and tags the next team member, passing off the clothespin. That player then runs down to the tent cards to find the second word of the verse, picking it up with the clothespin, and placing it on the designated line to the right of the one already there. Play continues until the teams complete their verse.

VISUAL RECORDING

Needed:

- video camera

Using a video camera is most beneficial when the learner thinks they have mastered a Scripture, or are getting really close. Videotape them against a plain background and without cues from you.

Many times, we think we're doing something one way, but when we see a recording, we're astounded at how different we're coming across. The kids will be able to recognize on their own that they are saying it so fast that no one could possibly understand, that there are places where the pause seems like an hour has passed as they search for the next trigger, or they've been using an incorrect word. It's a great tool for self-evaluation for visual learners.

WINDOW SHADES

Needed:

- black permanent marker
- old window shades

This is a great activity to use with a class when they are trying to memorize 3 or more verses. Roll out an old window shade and write the entire verse on the inside. If you can mount the shade, it's even more fun. Some handy guy should be able to make you a mount that doesn't even need a window!

Pull the shade all the way down when the kids are just beginning to learn the verse. As you sense they have mastered a line or two, raise the window shade to hide what they already have memorized. Each session they have together, they will want to raise the shade. The object is to get the shade all the way up so the sun will shine in!

Keep these shades and display them once a year in the hallways of your church to show the congregation all the Scriptures the kids now have hidden in their hearts. If you have an "Open House", it would be fun to station a kid at each of the shades to recite the Scripture as the adult(s) follow along on their cheat-sheet-shade.

Notes:

_____

_____

_____

_____

_____

_____

_____

_____

_____

_____

_____

_____

_____

_____

_____

RECALL Games & Activities

When you are repeating a Scripture over and over, you are engaging one part of your brain. The Scripture is in short-term memory. That's just a start! Please don't stop there.

When you play a game—moving your body and interacting with others—a different part of the brain is engaged. When you move back and forth between repeating and recalling utilizing something fun like games, you're strengthening the way your brain finds the Scripture and recalls it. Each time you interrupt the repeating of the verse with an action (like in a game), the brain has to figure out where it put that verse when you're asked to go back and say it. This gives the learner lots of exercise in recalling the Scripture, because he has to remember his trigger and use it to lead him into the verse.

The following games are designed to briefly interrupt the repeating process so the brain has no choice but to be strengthened as it tries to recall. This recalling is instrumental in moving the Scripture into long-term memory.

BALANCING ACT

Needed:

- Hymnals/books

If you have old hymnals stored somewhere, get them out for the kids to use in this exercise. Give each player a hymnal and tell them to line up across one end of the room. At the signal, the players will place the books on their heads and begin walking across the room, continuing to balance the book. When the leader says, "CHANGED!" then they will change directions and walk backwards. Each time the leader says "CHANGED", the players will change directions they are walking. The first kid to reach the other side of the room…and still have the book on his head…will recall the memory verse or lead his group in reciting it.

BOWLING

Needed:

- masking tape

- play bowling set

Mark a stand-behind line with the masking tape. Set up a play bowling set about 15 feet away. The player will roll the ball and count the number of pins that fell down. They can then choose that number of kids to recite the memory verse with them.

For a giant twist to this game, use a Giant Bowling Set (hearthsong.com). The kids love playing with this giant inflatable set! Check it out, 'cause it's a blast!

CARRY THE QUARTER

Needed:

- quarters

Each player will have a quarter. At the signal, the player will carry the quarter to a designated place and back, BUT the way they carry it will be different for each round.

Carry the quarter on the end of an index finger.

Carry the quarter on your forehead.

Carry the quarter on the top of your shoe.

Carry the quarter on your forearm.

Carry the quarter on your elbow.

Carry the quarter on your shoulder.

Carry the quarter on the end of your pinkie finger.

Carry the quarter on your cheek.

The player who returns to the starting line first will say the Scripture or lead their group in saying the Scripture together. Choose a new player for each round.

CATCH THE MARSHMALLOW

Needed:

- large plastic cups

- pancake turners (spatulas)

- masking tape

- regular size marshmallows

Using masking tape, mark 2 parallel lines on the floor about 8-feet apart. The kids will play in pairs and face one another, standing on the tape lines. One person in each pair will hold a large plastic cup. The other person will have a supply of marshmallows and a pancake turner.

When the signal is given, the player with the pancake turner will place one marshmallow on it. Then, holding the very end of the pancake turner, they have to toss the marshmallow at their partner, who will try to catch the marshmallow in their cup. When one pair gets 3 marshmallows in their cup, play stops, and that pair recites the Scripture.

FLICKER

Needed:

- buckets

- pennies

- rectangular table(s)

The number of kids who can play at the same time depends on the amount of space you have on rectangular tables. The kids who are playing will line up along one side of the table. All the other kids will line up behind these to make up their teams. On the floor on the opposite side of the table from each child should be a bucket. Give all the players a supply of pennies.

At the signal, the players on one side of the table will lay one of their pennies down on their table edge and flick it. Flicking is done by pulling back the index finger with the thumb and then letting it go. They players try to flick the penny across the table so that it goes off the opposite table edge and drops in the bucket. The first player to successfully get 3 pennies in his or her bucket will lead his or her team in saying the Scripture together.

HALO TOSS

Needed:

- cheap rope tinsel
- hot glue
- scissors

Cut some gold tinsel into lengths about 2 feet long. Slightly overlap the ends and use a hot glue gun to join the ends to make a tinsel circle. It's really a halo! Make a supply of these.

Choose some pairs of kids to play. Each pair will stand about 6 feet apart. At the signal, one person from each pair will toss their halos one at a time and the other person will try to get the tossed halo to stay on his or her head. The first pair to get the halo to stay on will recite the Scripture together. Continue playing with new pairs.

IT'S A WEDDING

Needed:

- fake wedding bouquet

At weddings the bride throws the bouquet. Whoever catches it is supposed to be the next person to get married. Well, we're not going to choose who gets married next, but we are going to choose whose team says the memory verse. We'll choose by tossing a fake bouquet.

You can make a fake bouquet by stapling gift bows on a piece of poster board and tying some ribbons to hang from the bottom. Think of something you may have seen at a wedding shower. Form groups of any number that you like. Choose one child to be the "bride." Each team will send one representative to be in the group that gets to try to catch the bouquet. Give the bride the bouquet and have them turn their back to the group that will catch. Try to keep the catching group from clustering together. There will be no signal. The bride can throw the bouquet over his or her shoulder anytime they choose. The person who catches the bouquet will lead his or her group in saying the memory verse together.

The person who caught the bouquet will now become the "bride" to toss for the next round. The teams will all send a new representative to try to catch the bouquet.

LONDON BRIDGE

This activity is especially good with younger children memorizing simpler verses. Two people will make the bridge, and the rest of the group will line up. Those in the line will progress under the bridge as everyone sings to the tune of "London Bridge," only they'll use the words:

My friends and I will learn God's Word,

Learn God's Word,

Learn God's Word,

My friends and I will learn God's Word,

I can say this verse.

The two making the bridge collapse their arms around the person who is under the arch at that time. That child will say the verse. If they have difficulty, then give them the opportunity to ask a classmate for help.

POSSESSION

Needed:

- flash cards

Write each word of the verse to be memorized on a separate card. There should be enough so that each child participating will have at least one card. Spread the cards out on the ground in a large area at the end of an open room. Choose one child to guard the cards. The other children will try to take possession of one card at a time without getting tagged by the guard.

When a player gets a card without being caught by the guard, they must say the entire verse and then take the card to the other end of the room to a holding pen before returning to try to get another card. Continue until all the cards are now in the possession of the children. If there are players who did not get a card, others who have extras should give away a card. Now, put the verse together by having each child say the word he or she has on a card as it is time for it to be said. This becomes a verbal puzzle. Say it again a little faster. The kids will enjoy trying to see how fast they can actually say the entire verse without getting words tangled.

SKATEBOARDING

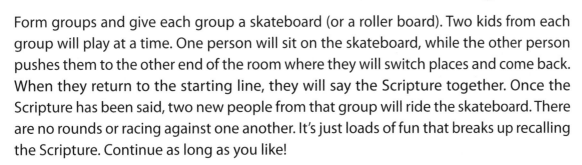

Needed:

- skateboards

Form groups and give each group a skateboard (or a roller board). Two kids from each group will play at a time. One person will sit on the skateboard, while the other person pushes them to the other end of the room where they will switch places and come back. When they return to the starting line, they will say the Scripture together. Once the Scripture has been said, two new people from that group will ride the skateboard. There are no rounds or racing against one another. It's just loads of fun that breaks up recalling the Scripture. Continue as long as you like!

SKEE BALL

Needed:

- 3 colors of poster board
- marker
- masking tape
- pennies
- stapler

You're going to create something like a skeetball game. Cut 4" strips of three different colors of poster board the full length of the sheet. Staple 2 pieces of the same color, end-to-end. Then, staple the ends to make a circle. Do the same thing with a second color of poster board, only cut about 6" off one of the strips before stapling the ends together. Repeat this process with the third color of poster board, but cut 12" off one piece (or basically cut it in half). Then staple the ends of the strips together to make 3 circles. These will stand up and can be positioned inside one another (much like a skeetball game). On the outside ring write "3", on the middle ring write "2", and on the smallest inside ring write "1".

With a piece of masking tape indicate a stand-behind line. The kids will take turns tossing a penny at the nested strips. The number on the outside of the ring indicates how many people the tosser will recruit to say the memory verse with him if he gets the penny to land inside that ring. So, if the penny lands inside the ring marked "3", then the tosser will choose 3 other people to join him in reciting the memory verse. Continue playing in this manner, repeating the verse in varied sizes of groups, each time a penny lands inside a skeetball ring.

STACK 'EM UP

Needed:

- cardstock

- large plastic cups

Each player will need 4 large plastic cups and 3 pieces of cardstock cut in 4" squares. At the signal the players will race to see who can make a tower by alternating setting a cup upside down on the table, piece of cardstock on top of it, cup, cardstock, cup, cardstock, and cup. The first person to complete their tower will say the Scripture or lead their team in reciting it.

STICKY SITUATION

Needed:

- cardboard

- paper towels

- petroleum jelly

- ping-pong balls

You need a hard floor for this game (no carpet). Each person will need an 8-inch square of cardboard. Put a thick layer of petroleum jelly all over one side of the cardboard and place it on the floor about 8-feet from the stand-behind line. Give each player a supply of ping-pong balls. At the signal, the players will bounce one ball at a time at the cardboard. The objective is to get the ping-pong ball to stick in the petroleum jelly, but it must bounce at least one time before landing on the cardboard. The first person to get a ball to stick in their cardboard will recite the verse.

Have some paper towels handy to wipe off balls that have gotten stuck in the petroleum jelly, so they can return to play.

THROUGH THE HULA HOOP

Needed:

- 2-foot pieces of PVC pipe

- hula hoop

- string

- tennis balls

Give each player a 2-foot piece of PVC and a tennis ball. Hang a hula hoop about 10-feet off the ground. The hula hoop should be at least 20-feet away from the players.

The players will hold the PVC by one end so that the pipe is vertical. Rest a tennis ball on the opposite end from the one the kid is holding. At the signal, all these players will move toward the hula hoop, keeping the tennis ball balanced on the end of the PVC. Once they reach the hula hoop, they must raise the PVC until they can get the ball to go through the hoop. The first player to do this, in each round, will lead their group in reciting the Scripture memory verse.

TOSS IT

Needed:

- medium-size playground ball or a large Koosh® ball

A soft, squishy ball works best, because it is easier for the children to catch and control. You don't want a ball that is difficult to catch because it will slow the rhythm of the recitation.

With the leader in the center, assemble a tight circle surrounding him/her. The closer the circle, the more control the children will keep of the ball, which means the game will flow more smoothly. Start the memory verse by saying the Scripture reference and the first word of the verse. Throw a ball to one of the kids, and he or she will say the next word. The child throws it back to you, and you say the third word. Throw to another kid, and he or she says the fourth word, and so on. The ball needs to come back to the leader in the center each throw, so the leader can retain control of the group and the verse.

TWISTER®

Needed:

- Twister® mat(s)

You will need a Twister® mat for every four players. Groups of four will form around each mat. This Scripture memorization game is played with the traditional Twister® game that uses a spinner. Each time the spinner spins, a command is given with a color (red, blue, green, yellow) and a part of the body (right foot, left foot, right hand, left hand). All the players place their foot or hand on the appropriate color of dot each time the spinner stops and are not allowed to move that foot or hand until another command is given for it. The command that the children are especially listening for is the right foot command. Anytime the spinner chooses a color for the right foot, all the players must recite the Scripture from memory while moving their foot into position.

WHATCHA GONNA DO?

Needed:

- 15 pieces of copier paper
- container
- music that can be paused
- objects that can have numbers written on them

This works best in a very large room or gym. Number some tokens (such as craft sticks, corks, Bingo chips, rocks) with the numbers 1-15. Place the tokens in a container. Number pieces of copy paper (8½" x 11") with the numbers 1-15, then add any additional pieces if you have more than 15 kids playing, so there will be a piece of paper for each child. On the underside of the numbered pieces of paper, write actions like:

Walk like a duck

Pat your head and scratch your knee

Hop on one foot

Spin in circles

Tiptoe around the room

Say as fast as you can

Say in whale talk … s-l-o-w-l-y

Whisper

Walk backwards

Jog in place

Put your head on the floor

Shout while marching

Walk around on your knees

Twirl like a ballerina

To start the game, the children run around the room while music plays. When the music stops, each child moves to a piece of paper to stand on. Draw a numbered token from the container and call out the number. Whoever is standing on the paper with that number will turn the paper over and read what is written on the other side. Everyone will do what the paper says while they say the verse together. So, if the paper says, "Walk like a duck," then everyone walks around the room holding their ankles, walking like a duck while they say the memory verse. If no one is standing on the number called, draw another until you match up with someone. Once a number is called, remove the paper and the token from the game, so it cannot be called again.

WHO HAS THE PENNIES?

Needed:

- pennies

The children will sit in a circle with their hands behind their backs. One child is chosen to stand in the middle with his or her eyes closed. Stop peeking! I see you! The teacher will place a penny in the hands of three of the children. (This number can vary according to the size of your group.)

The person in the middle opens his or her eyes and guesses three people who he thinks has a penny in their hands. If he is correct in any of his choices, then the people who have been found with the pennies must stand and say their verse. A new person is chosen for the middle, and the person who was in the middle secretly puts the three pennies in the hands of the new players.

REVIEW Games and Activities

One of the big mistakes of Scripture memorization is thinking that the verse is in long-term memory once you can say it through without help. You HAVE to review periodically, or the verse will fade from memory. The more verses you know, the easier it is to get them confused or forget parts.

In the church setting, we're guilty of presenting a different verse to kids every week. We think by devoting 5 minutes to its memorization the verse is actually in their memories. That's far from the truth!

One of the biggest challenges for keeping Scripture secured in the memory is to review and sort through the verses. It will quickly become evident what is really committed to memory and what is lost in gray matter never-never land.

These games will provide a way to evaluate how well the Scriptures were memorized by reviewing a group of verses at the same time. Engage kids by making this review fun, utilizing play.

CANDY GRAB

Needed:

- small wrapped candies

Choose 2 kids to play against one another. They will stand facing one another with their hands behind their backs. The leader will stand between them with one hand extended. On the leader's open, flattened hand will be one piece of wrapped candy.

At the signal, the kids will see who can grab the candy out of the leader's hand first. The person who is now holding the candy will say the verse that's "up for grabs" or lead their group in saying it.

CUBE TOSS

Needed:

- 2 square facial tissue boxes

- clear tape

- glue stick

- marker

- photos of kids

- plain wrapping paper

For the 2 cubes, you can use the square facial tissue boxes (or you can buy plastic photo cubes). Wrap both boxes with plain wrapping paper. Then, glue pictures of the kids in your class on all 6 sides of the box. You can put one kid on each side or multiples on each side. When this cube is tossed, it will determine who is going to say the verse.

The second box is going to be the box that determines which verse is recited. Write one verse on each side of the box.

Choose a child to toss the photo cube and a different child to toss the Scripture cube. The children pictured on the side that lands up will say the Scripture that lands up on the Scripture cube. After they recite it together (or individually, depending on how many photos you put on the sides), then choose 2 new kids to toss the cubes.

PUSH IT HERE, PUSH IT THERE

Needed:

- index cards

- marker

- paint stir sticks

This can be used for one verse or multiple verses that you're reviewing. Let's talk about how to do it with multiple verses, and you'll catch on how to do it with a single verse.

Determine the set of Scriptures you want to review. Write the address of each one on a separate index card and place those cards on the floor several feet apart from one another. Then, write each Scripture on a set of index cards, but not individual words. Instead, write chunks or phrases on each card, so that each verse has 4-6 cards. Mix all these cards together and place them, words up, on the floor in a central location.

Give the kids a paint stir stick. At the signal, they will start moving the cards to the Scripture address they go with and assembling the verses in order…but they can only move the cards by scooting them with the paint stir stick.

Now, isn't this a lot more fun than just sitting and saying the verses over and over?

RUBBER BAND MATCH

Needed:

- hammer
- large rubber bands
- nails
- piece of plywood

On a board write different Scripture addresses down a left-hand column. In a different order write the verses in a right-hand column. Put a nail at the end of each Scripture address and another nail at the beginning of each verse written out.

The children will attach rubber bands from the nail next to the Scripture address to its matching verse.

SHAKE IT UP

Needed:

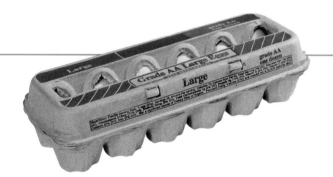

- egg carton
- fine-point marker
- marble

Write the addresses of 12 verses that you've learned inside each well of an egg carton. You can do this as a group, one child at a time, or give each child her or his own egg carton for practice.

Place a marble in the egg carton and close it. Now, shake the egg carton and hold onto it until you can tell the marble has come to rest in an egg well. When the child opens the egg carton, wherever the marble lands is the verse he or she must recite.

Put this activity in your *Mosey-In* file of activities kids can do while you're waiting for everyone to arrive—waiting for everyone to mosey in.

TOPPLE

Needed:

- beanbags
- funnel
- permanent marker
- sand
- water bottles

When reviewing several verses that you've memorized, sometimes the hardest part is remembering the Scripture address. Try this little game to work on that.

Using a funnel, add about 1/8-cup of sand to some empty water bottles. Cap them tightly. Write the first 3 words of each verse you are reviewing on separate bottles using a permanent marker. Set these along a wall, out from the baseboard a little, and about 6 inches apart.

Determine a stand-behind line using a rope or some masking tape. Each child, on his or her turn, will toss 3 beanbags at the water bottles. If a bottle topples, the leader will read the 3 words written on that bottle. Then, the child uses those trigger words to recall the Scripture address. If the child gets it correct, remove the water bottle from the line-up. If he doesn't, then return the bottle to its place for another player to knock over.

WHEEL OF SCRIPTURE

Needed:

- markers
- cardboard pizza board
- ruler
- spinner apparatus

Create a spinner using a pizza board. Determine the center of the pizza board and place a dot there. Use a ruler to draw lines across the board going through that dot. This will divide the pizza board into sections. Don't feel like the slices need to be identical. In fact, it's a little more fun when they aren't. Poke a hole through the dot and insert the spinner apparatus. (You can purchase these little spinners at a teacher supply store, usually several in one package.)

Color the slices, or make each slice look like a different kind of pizza. Now, on the individual slices write the Scripture address for the verses you are reviewing. You can give point values to the kinds of pizza: pepperoni is worth 50 points, sausage worth 100 points, mushroom and green peppers worth 200 points, and a plain cheese worth 250 points (because that's my favorite). Include several slices of each kind of pizza on the board.

The players will take turns pizza spinning and then reciting the verse the spinner lands on. If they are successful, they receive the number of points their pizza was worth.

If you're ambitious and would like to make a spinner on steroids, then go online and get instructions for making one out of PVC pipe, or contact Gary Gramlich at thefungroup1273@gmail.com

MY SCRIPTURE MEMORIZATION LOG

As you memorize Scripture, it's fun to keep a log so you can look back at what Scripture was memorized and when you completed it. This also helps as you review all previously memorized Scripture. On the log, you'll want to note the Scripture address, the date memorized, and mark the verse(s) that you're presently working on.

It's easy to keep a log like this in your computer. But, if you're motivated by visuals, then noting these on a poster or on individual sticky notes in a well-traveled place will be inspiration to keep going…and that cheerleader reminding you of what you've accomplished.

In addition, in one of your Bibles highlight and date all verses that you've memorized. What a keepsake and wonderful tool to show your kids, grandkids, or friends to encourage them in this spiritual discipline.

Notes:

_____

_____

_____

_____

_____

_____

_____

_____

_____

_____

Working on it	Scripture Address	Date Memorized
❏	Genesis 1:1	Sept. 1
❏	Exodus 20:2	Sept. 4
❏	Leviticus 20:7-8	Sept. 8
❏	Numbers 6:24-26	Sept. 12
❏	Deuteronomy 6:4-5	Sept. 16
❏	Joshua 1:9	Sept. 20
❏	Judges 17:6	Sept. 25
❏	Ruth 1:16	Oct. 1
❏	1 Samuel 8:5	Oct. 6
❏	2 Samuel 7:16	Oct. 11
❏	1 Kings 11:11	Oct. 16
❏	2 Kings 23:27	Oct. 22
❏	1 Chronicles 29:11	Oct. 27
❏	2 Chronicles 7:14	Nov. 2
❏	Ezra 3:11	Nov. 8
❏	Nehemiah 2:17	Nov. 14
❏	Esther 4:14	Nov. 19
❏	Job 19:25	Nov. 27
❏	Psalms 100:4	Dec. 2
❏	Proverbs 3:5-6	Dec. 8
❏	Ecclesiastes 7:20	Dec. 15
❏	Song of Solomon 2:4	Dec. 22
❏	Isaiah 53:11	Dec. 30
❏	Jeremiah 33:3	Jan. 8
❏	Lamentations 3:22-23	Jan 18
❏	Ezekiel 37:27-28	Jan 23
❏	Daniel 2:21	Jan 30

Notes:

Notes:

Part Three

Intensive 6-week Program

Raising the Bar

When my friend Dave felt God's call to the mission field, a crucial reality hit him. He realized that under adverse conditions there was a possibility that one day his precious Bible might be taken from him. If he were suddenly unable to turn the pages of the books, chapters, and verses he went to for answers, guidance, and inspiration, what would he do? That was indeed a valid consideration, and Dave's response came straight from Psalm 119:11 (NLT), *I have hidden your word in my heart, that I might not sin against you*. Dave's solution was to memorize Scripture, book by book, and hide it in a place where no one could take it away. No government would find it under a board in the floor. No doctor could cut it from his body. No soldier could rip it from his hands to throw into a burning pile. God's Word was written in Dave's heart, scratched into his brain, and branded into his soul.

I shared my friend's story in children's church one Sunday and had no idea what impact it had made on those little listeners. Some time later, eight children encircled me, united with a request, "We want to memorize Scripture." When I responded that we do memorize our theme Scriptures to go along with lessons, I was quickly derailed. Another spokes-child chimed in, "No, we want to memorize like your friend." Eight children had been challenged to memorize large portions of Scripture, and they wanted some help. My reaction went two directions. First, I was thrilled that they wanted to tackle such a huge undertaking, but then I was disappointed in myself because I had failed to set the bar high enough for these kids. They were setting their own bar.

Their challenge became my challenge. How do you teach, really teach, kids to memorize this amount of Scripture? I searched for resources, and nothing I found offered help outside of memorizing random verses. Consequently, I drew on my experience as a children's pastor, my understanding of child development, and my personal relationship with each child. Keeping in mind that this was an enormous undertaking for these kids, I refused to water down the challenge even though I had my doubts of how successful we would be.

Life is a series of challenges, and that's the first thing the kids needed to understand. They needed to realize that we overcome some challenges and we fall short of others, but the one common ground for facing every challenge is that we tackle it with everything we've been given by God. That includes our intelligence, our enthusiasm, our strengths, our weaknesses, our likes, and our dislikes. Each one is a tool and using those tools properly will certainly increase the odds for positive outcomes.

The kids had voiced a big challenge—a challenge that few adults ever take on, so the enormity of what they wanted to do needed to become real to each one. Conveying that did not come in a few encouraging words, but needed reinforcing continuously from parents, leadership, and the congregation. It became apparent that one responsibility of the adult leader is to be the **MOTIVATOR**. That adult is the head cheerleader, responsible for noticing each little success and applauding it in some way. As a motivator, he or she must persistently be looking for signs of success and ways to spur that child on by reminding him of the goal and why he is involved.

Another responsibility of the lead adult is to **MONITOR**. Learning a lengthy passage doesn't happen overnight, so keep an eye on each child's progress. If he or she gets behind, offer ways of catching up, and make accountability more frequent. Can you imagine how excited a child would be if you called in the middle of the week for the sole purpose of hearing him or her say what was learned so far? It's not just a reminder to the child, but it also becomes a reminder to the parent to monitor the child's progress.

The third key responsibility of the leader is to introduce **METHODS** that will make possible a successful ending. Keep in mind, the more variety of multiple intelligences that are utilized, the more complete the understanding of the passage will be. They'll also have a lot more fun in the process! It's obvious that memorizing Scripture taps into the word smart, but what activities actually do that and what about the other multiple intelligences? Let's make use of all the smarts—all our resources—and incorporate word, picture, music, math, nature, body, self, and people smarts.

Memorizing large portions of Scripture is not an adult discipline; in fact, it won't become an adult discipline if we overlook laying the foundation for it in our children. Don't discount what your children are capable of. When the Bible tells us that "a little child will lead," it could be that children can set the standard for memorizing Scripture. They may raise the bar for adults!

Notes:

_____

_____

_____

_____

_____

_____

_____

_____

Notes:

Lesson Plan: Week #1

Opening

Find an oil lamp that you can use each week, and a large Bible that will be marked with Psalm 119:105. Each of the children will look up Psalm 119:105 at the first meeting. Provide the same version of the Bible for them and read it in unison. ***What does this verse call the Word of God? It calls it a light and a lamp. This is going to be our theme verse. We are learning God's Word, which is a lamp that shows us how to live.*** Explain that there are three things you will do each week as you open the session.

- You will light your lamp.
- You will open the Bible to Psalm 119:105 and say the verse together.
- You will sing a song, "Thy Word Is a Lamp," which is Psalm 119:105 to music.

If you haven't already done so, give your group a name. We liked to call this special group the Lamplighters.

Assign Verses

Beforehand, choose an assortment of Scripture passages that the children can select from. (We've included a list of longer passages, but you're not limited to that.) Make sure there is a variety in length of Scripture passages and difficulty of vocabulary as consideration for the differences in your students' learning abilities, age, support at home, time commitment, and willingness.

Print out each passage, double-spaced, and laminate each one. **It is important to laminate them!** (If you do not have a heat laminator for 9" x 12" paper, it's an investment of about $40 and is one of the best resources you can have around.) Give the children plenty of time to browse through the Scriptures to choose which one they would like to accept as their challenge. Allowing them to make their choice immediately gives them ownership in the process. Your goal is for children to experience success in accomplishing the memorization of their passage—especially the first time to memorize this way. Encourage the child not to over-commitment.

You will want to write down the child's name and the Scripture passage he or she has chosen for future reference.

Introduce Key to Memorization #1

Talk with the kids about Key to Memorization #1—Get It Right—found in the front section of this book on page 7. As they begin to memorize their passage, they will need to be conscious that every word matters. They need to make sure that what they are memorizing is exactly what is in the verse. This is the Word of God we are memorizing, and we do not want to change even one word of it.

Highlight Vocabulary

Needed:

- highlighters

Give children a highlighter to mark three words in their passage that they are not familiar with. As homework this week, they will find out what these words mean and how they help make sense of the verse.

PLAY HOT POTATO

The children will sit in a circle and pass a potato (or other object like a beanbag) around the circle as the music plays. When the music stops, the person holding the potato states the Scripture address to the passage they have chosen.

PLAY FILL THE BUCKET

Needed:

- buckets
- masking tape
- newspaper

Provide each kid with an ice cream bucket (or other large container, such as a classroom garbage can or a large kettle).

The containers need to be very similar in size.

Before the game begins the kids will wad up half sheets of newspaper to make about 20 small tight balls each.

Place the buckets against the wall and put masking tape down about 8 feet from the buckets.

Set a timer for three minutes; then give the signal.

Each player will toss his or her paper wads at the bucket; everyone tossing at the same time. When a player gets a paper wad in the bucket, he has to yell out the Scripture address before he can continue to toss his other paper wads. Continue tossing until the timer goes off. (Players will have to retrieve their own paper wads, unless you want to play 2 rounds and have half the kids retrieving for their partner.) The players will count the number of paper wads they got into their bucket. If you choose to do so, give the winner a token prize.

Homework

Pass out the homework assignment and review what the children are to do this week.

Week 1: Homework Assignment

Find out what the 3 words you highlighted in your Scripture mean. Look in the dictionary and ask others. Be ready to tell the group next week what one of your words means.

Ask 3 adults to read your Scripture passage and then ask them what they think it means. Be ready to share with a coach a little about this next week.

Memorize the Scripture address and the first two sentences.

Notes:

_____

_____

_____

_____

_____

_____

_____

_____

_____

_____

_____

Notes:

Lesson Plan: Week #2

- Opening Exercises
- Light the lamp
- Open the Bible to Psalm 119:105
- Choose one of the children to lead the group in reciting Psalm 119:105
- Sing "Thy Word Is a Lamp"

Find Your Balloon

Needed:

- balloons for all the kids (all the same color)
- black permanent marker
- music

It's important that all balloons be the same color, and lighter color balloons work best. Once the kids have chosen their Scripture passage, you will write the reference (Scripture address) on a balloon. All the kids will hold a balloon at the beginning, and it doesn't matter whose balloon it is. Play some music, and while the music is playing, the kids can go completely bonkers, batting the balloons around. When the music stops, they have to locate the balloon that has their Scripture address on it. This will help them identify the address visually. Continue to play the music, bat the balloons, and find your balloon.

Instruction Time

Help the kids understand the challenge of memorizing Scripture.

What are your distractions? (TV, siblings, music)

Each kid needs to identify what things will compete for his attention when he's trying to work on his memorization. Give children an opportunity to verbalize this to one another. This will help with accountability also. Satan will try to get them off track, so they need to be aware of the distractions that will be a temptation. Identifying these weak places will give them the ammunition to fight back.

Reclaim a certain time to set aside for Scripture memorization.

Decide when you will work on your Scripture memorization for 10 minutes each day. Tell all family members what your intention is and ask them to respect that time. Family members can also encourage the memorizer and hold him or her accountable.

Watch out for pride.

Do not think yourself better than any of the other kids because your passage is longer or you memorized quicker.

Exaggerate when you say it.

Say the verse in a variety of ways that seem very exaggerated. If you're going to say the verse **fast**, then say it as fast as you possibly can. If you're going to say it in a **whisper**, then make it barely audible. Shout big words or words that you have difficulty pronouncing.

PLAY HOPSCOTCH

Needed:

- masking tape

Create a hopscotch grid on the floor with masking tape. The blocks of the grid should measure 12"-18". You will need one playing grid for each 4 children. The kids will take turns jumping through the hopscotch blocks, saying one or two words of their verse with each hop. They will go as far as they have learned and then stop hopping. The leaders will need to keep copies of the verses handy to prompt the kids if they get stuck in a place where they thought they knew the verse.

This is not as easy as it may sound. They are coordinating a physical motion that takes their concentration and an intellectual exercise that takes a lot of concentration…at the same time. Their brains have to move quickly back and forth between tasks. It's a great exercise for brain health, but it is difficult. (If you can, leave the hopscotch grids down for the next couple of weeks. You'll find that the kids will do this exercise when they are in the building at other times of the week.) You can also purchase indoor/outdoor hopscotch mats from websites such as hearthsong.com for about $40.

Introduce Key to Memorization #3

Go to the Keys to Memorization section of this book and talk with the kids about how understanding unfamiliar vocabulary will help them with their memorization.

Share Vocabulary Study

One of the homework assignments from this past week was that each child was to find out the meaning of three words in their Scripture—words they are not familiar with. Create small groups of about 5 or 6 kids. (See suggestion below on a fun and yummy

ways to decide on groups.) A coach is needed for each of the groups. The kids will share about the three words they did a vocabulary search on this week. Then, give each child an opportunity to share the meaning of one of the words with the rest of the group. They will be sharing the meanings of other words in the weeks to come.

PLAY FLASHLIGHT TAG

Needed:

- black landscape plastic
- flashlight

Beforehand, create as dark a room as possible. Cover any glass where light could come in with heavy black landscape plastic. (You can get rolls of this at Walmart or at a home improvement store.) Give a flashlight to one child and put him/her in the middle of the room. Turn out the lights, so the room is completely dark. The person with the flashlight doesn't move, but when she or he says, "go," everyone else moves about the room slowly. Remember, *slowly* because it's dark! The players are not allowed to hide behind anything and must remain standing. The flashlight person calls out "Your Word is my light!" and everyone freezes. Then, the flashlight is turned on.

If the flashlight is not pointing at someone directly, then the holder of the flashlight will move slowly in one direction until a player is in the light. That person then says as much of their memory verse as they can without any prompting. Then, they become the holder of the flashlight, and the game goes into round two. If the flashlight shines on someone who has already said his or her verse, keep moving the flashlight until it lands on someone who hasn't.

SHARE VERSE MEANINGS

Needed:

- timer

It is crucial that you respect the fact that children completed the homework you gave them for the week by following up on it during the meeting time. Kids who don't want to do school homework will surprise you and do this Scripture homework. It's a novelty, so it doesn't feel like their regular routine homework.

You will need to break the kids into two groups. You can do that by tossing a beanbag at the hopscotch game. The first half of the kids who get the beanbag to land on the #4 or #5 square are on one team. The others who did not get a beanbag to land on the #4 or #5 square will be the second group.

This past week for homework each child was supposed to ask three adults what they thought his or her verse meant. Give each child 30 seconds to share as much as she or he can about their verse. Keep a timer going so the kids get the idea of how long this amount of time is. This seems like a short amount of time to an adult, but it will be plenty of time for the children.

CATEGORIZE PASSAGES

Needed:

- index cards
- tape
- wide marker

Beforehand, prepare cards with the Scripture addresses on them, so that each child will have his verse written on a card. Put signs up on the wall: Praise, Instruction, Testimonial, Conversation with God, Other. Explain that Scriptures serve different purposes and what these categories mean. Some passages are all about praising God. Others seem to be prayers or conversations with God. Some are telling others what the Lord has done—a testimonial. But, all of them are worth memorizing. These are big words, but allow the children an opportunity to try and figure out what kinds of Scriptures might fall in these categories. One at a time, the kids will tape their card under the category sign that applies to their verse and give a brief explanation as to why they put it there. Don't worry if the verses that are assigned are weighted in one area. If one area is not covered, ask the children to look up a verse that falls in that category.

*Suggestion for breaking into groups

Needed:

- Hershey's® Kisses,
- container

Beforehand, purchase a package of Hershey's® Kisses that are wrapped in a variety of colors. These are easy to find around holidays. Place the same number of Kisses as there are kids in a container, dividing the colors equally into the number of groups you want to make. Pass the Kisses out to the children quickly and tell them not to eat the candy, yet. Once the groups are formed according to color, the children can eat their treat. The same thing can be done with M&M'S® or Skittles®.

Homework

Remind the children that they will be sharing one more vocabulary word definition next week, along with anything else they would like to add from their interviews on the meaning of the verses.

Stress to the children that the Scripture passages cannot be learned by working on them only at the weekly meetings. They must work on them at home. Give each child a days-of-the-week card where they can cross off each day when they spend 10 minutes working on their passage.

Your Challenge

- Get away from ALL distractions
- Get out your passage.
- Set a timmer for 10 minutes and devote the time to memorizing.
- Mark off each day that you meet the challenge.
- return to next meeting.

Monday	Tuesday	Wednesday	Thursday

Friday	Saturday	Sunday

Notes:

Lesson Plan: Week #3

Opening

- Light the lamp
- Open the Bible to Psalm 119:105
- Recite Psalm 119:105 together
- Sing "Thy Word Is a Lamp"

Share Vocabulary

Each child will be given the opportunity to share the meaning of another one of the difficult words they chose from their Scripture passage.

HOPSCOTCH

Repeat the hopscotch game from last week. This will give the children something familiar to begin with, and hopefully, they can go further than they went last week because they have more memorized. It's also a good activity for the kids as you wait for everyone to arrive. (See page 63)

MEMORY CARDS

Needed:

- cardstock hole puncher
- metal rings
- nametag-size labels

The children will make a set of memory cards. Beforehand, you will need to divide each verse into about 10 sections. Type or print each section on a label (name tag size). Give the children their set of Scripture labels and some cards made from quartering sheets of colored cardstock. (Index cards could also be used, but use the unlined ones.) All the cards for one particular Scripture should be the same color. This takes a while to prepare for the children, so don't wait until the last minute. It is, however, an invaluable and worthwhile tool to give them.

The children will stick each label on a card, then punch a hole, using a hole punch, in the upper left corner. Put these on a metal ring that you can purchase at any office supply store. The children can carry these cards with them to school or in the car. They can set goals of how many cards they will have memorized by next week.

Introduce Key to Memorization #4

Talk with the kids about Key to Memorization #4—breaking up the intensity. Explain that they can get the Scripture into long-term memory better when they say it, do something different for a few seconds, say the Scripture, do something different…back and forth. This forces them to locate the Scripture in their brain and recall it. It also keeps you from tiring of the memorization process so easily.

FOOTBALL GAME

Needed:

- 2 pieces of poster board
- 20 milk caps
- black permanent marker
- brown construction paper
- container

Use two pieces of poster board to create a football field, marking the 10-yard lines. On 20 milk bottle caps, write what will be the yardage (5, 10, 15, 20, 25, and 30). Make 4 each of the smaller numbers and two each of the 25 and 30. Place all the bottle caps in a container. Make a little construction paper football for each child and put his or her name on it.

Each time it is a player's turn, he or she will draw a bottle cap that tells how far the football can move if he or she answers correctly. Once that player has had a turn, return the cap to the container. During the first round of play, each player will pick a bottle cap that tells how many yards he or she will get to move for saying his or her Scripture address. In the second round players will choose a new bottle cap and say the first sentence of their Scripture passage. Then, in the third round, they pick a bottle cap and say their Scripture address…but, there's more! The leader will say the first sentence, and the player will try to add the second sentence. Repeat rounds one, two, and three until someone scores a touchdown.

INTRODUCE THE COMPLETION BOARD

Needed:

- Certificates

Use a bulletin board as a Completion Board. When a child thinks he or she can say his or her passage in its entirety to one of the coaches, then at the close of the session, the leader will have a completed certificate to put on the bulletin board. It's fun to make this a lighthearted, but serious at the same time, ceremony. You may want to place a mortarboard on the recipient.

Homework

Send home a fresh day-to-day tally card so kids can see their daily progress. Request that they return these cards each week. This way, you can evaluate their commitment and perhaps give some suggestions on how they can reclaim 10 minutes each day for their memorization.

We are excited to announce that

_____
(name)

has successfully memorized

_____
(Scripture address)

on _____.
(date)

CONGRATULATIONS!

Notes:

Lesson Plan: Week #4

Opening

- Light the lamp
- Open the Bible to Psalm 119:105
- Recite Psalm 119:105 together
- Sing "Thy Word Is a Lamp"

FIND A COACH

Needed:

- funny hats

The kids will need their laminated Scripture cards. Invite some adults to help for the first 10-15 minutes of your meeting time. Provide each one with a silly hat (or ask them to provide one), and then position him or her in random locations throughout the church. The kids will search for these silly-hatted coaches, hand them their laminated card, and recite as much of their passage as they can. Encourage the coaches to express some celebration about whatever each child was able to accomplish—with high fives, a silly little cheer, etc.

AUDIOTAPING

The children will be taken to a quiet place where they can tape record as much of their verse as they know. This can be done on a cell phone using an app like Voice Recorder. Replay it so they can hear how they did.

CLOTHESPIN FIND

Needed:

- ballpoint pen
- bucket
- spring clothespins

You will need a large supply of spring clothespins for this activity. Beforehand, choose six words, from each Scripture passage—unique to that passage. Make sure these words are not duplicated in any of the other verses or it will cause confusion in the activity. Write

81

each word on a separate clothespin with a ballpoint pen. Markers tend to bleed, even the fine-point ones. (If you have children learning the same Scripture, they will need to play with separate groups.) Place the clothespins from all the Scripture passages in one container. At "go" the leader will dump the entire container of clothespins on the floor. The children will try to find the 6 words that are in their verse. Each time they find one of their words, they will clip that clothespin to their clothes. The kids will then take turns saying their verse to a coach and removing the clothespins as they come across that word in their verse.

A TWIST TO HOPSCOTCH

Needed:

- bean bags

- hopscotch grid

Break into groups so that each hopscotch grid has no more than 4 children. Supply a beanbag at each grid. The child playing will toss the beanbag at any square. She will say her verse as she hops (as we have done previously). When she gets to the square with the beanbag on it, she has a decision to make. She has to decide if she can make it to the end and back to the beanbag, saying words to her verse, without missing any words. Each time she returns to the beanbag she has to make this decision. She can quit anytime she wants, but if she doesn't make it back, then she gets a point (and you don't want points!)

Introduce Key to Memorization #12

Talk with the kids about Key to Memorization #12—Utilizing the Multiple Intelligences. Multiple intelligences are all the ways you can take in information. You can do that through talking with other people, through words (reading them or hearing them), through music, and five more. One of those is through pictures. It is important to see your Scripture in some picture form, whether in a drawing, through a photograph, or through something you make with your hands.

PLAY-DOH®

Needed:

- supply of Play-Doh®

- wax paper

Give each child a piece of wax paper and access to Play-Doh®. Using the Play-Doh®, the children will express something about their verse. It can be an object from the verse or

something it makes them think of. Don't skip this activity, because it really engages the children who have different strengths. Give everyone an opportunity to share what they created from the Play-Doh® and how it relates to their passage.

I was once leery about using this activity because the group included lots of boys, especially one large "macho" football player. I was sure he would not appreciate playing with Play-Doh®. Surprisingly, his depiction of his Scripture passage was more detailed and had some extremely interesting abstract connections. On the other hand, the straight-A little girl who I thought would create something amazing presented her ball of blue Play-Doh® and said, "God made the earth."

Homework

Send home a fresh day-to-day tally card so that kids can keep track of days when they spent 10 minutes working on their passage.

Notes:

_____

_____

_____

_____

_____

_____

_____

_____

_____

_____

_____

Notes:

Lesson Plan: Week #5

Opening

- Light the lamp

- Open the Bible and say Psalm 119:105

- Recite Psalm 119:105 together

- Sing "Thy Word Is a Lamp"

FIND A COACH

Needed:

- adult listeners

- silly hats

Repeat this from last week. It is a phenomenal way of helping adults see how amazing the kids are and what huge memorization projects they are accomplishing. You can invite the same people from last week or get some new people to listen to the kids. Make sure they wear their silly hats, or have some other unique, fun identifying characteristic.

PLAY A MATCHING GAME

Needed:

- cardstock

Make 6 cards for each child's passage. Each card should have a phrase from the passage on it. Put all the cards (from all the verses) together and mix them up. Lay the cards face down on a table in rows. The kids will take turns turning over one card. They will read the card aloud so that everyone can hear it, and then decide if it is from their verse. If it is, they get to keep it. If it is not from their verse, they return it face down to the table. (The child who belongs to that phrase, though, will take note and be ready to turn it over on their turn.) The object is for each child to find the 6 cards from their verse.

Introduce Key to Memorization #8

Talk with the kids about Key to Memorization #8—Incorporate Music. Anything we put to music goes into long-term memory much, much, much easier than if we just try to say it. Think about all the songs you have memorized! Encourage the kids to think of their passages in terms of rhythm patterns or putting (at least parts of it) to music.

WRITE A SONG

You have the words! Now, all you have to do is connect them with a song. Post the titles of several familiar tunes where the children can easily see them. The entire passage does not need to be in the song, but pick out part of it to put to music. Important phrases can be repeated several times. Encourage them to make it their own!

PLAY BUZZ-IN

Beforehand, prepare a list of 5 phrases from each Scripture passage the children are memorizing. This game calls for a Quizzer (an electronic buzz-in device) if you have one. You can also use little tap-on lights found at dollar stores or counter bells, but make sure everyone has a device. You'll need some kind of object to "ring-in" with. The children will place their hands flat on the table with the buzzer in between their hands. The leader will read one of the phrases at random from the prepared list. The child who recognizes that phrase from his or her verse will buzz in and respond with the verse address.

MAKE PILLOWCASES

Needed:

- cardboard

- fabric markers

- pillowcases

Check local hotels for used pillowcases. Most hotels discard them on a routine basis. Wash the pillowcases, but do not use fabric softener. Place a piece of cardboard inside the pillowcase so that fabric paints will not bleed through. The kids will use fabric markers on the pillowcases to portray something about their verses.

These make wonderful keepsakes to commemorate their accomplishment of completing this 6-week intensive on Scripture memorization.

VIDEOTAPING

Needed:

- method of videotaping

This is a powerful tool! Provide an opportunity for the children who feel ready or would like additional practice to videotape during this session. (The main videotaping will be done next week.) It is best to pull the children out one-by-one and go to a separate quiet area where they can stand against a plain wall. Putting a marker on the floor where the

child should stand also helps. Some may earn their Certificate of Completion, so make sure you post their certificate on the bulletin board.

Needed:

- copies of group's unique word search

Prepare a word search containing the first names of all the kids. They work on these Scriptures as a group, and this is just a fun way of reinforcing the group camaraderie. You can make these on www.puzzlemaker.com for free.

Homework

Send home a fresh day-by-day tally sheet. We're getting close to the end, so help the children figure out how much time they may need to commit to memorizing this last week.

Notes:

_____

_____

_____

_____

_____

_____

_____

_____

_____

_____

Notes:

Lesson Plan: Week #6

Opening Exercises

- Light the lamp

- Open Bible and say Psalm 119:105

- Recite Psalm 119:105 together

- Sing "Thy Word Is a Lamp"

PLAY WITH BALLOONS

Needed:

- balloons all the same color

- permanent black marker

Write each Scripture address on a balloon, preferably all balloons are the same color. This way, each child has a balloon with her or his Scripture address on it to begin playing with. Bat the balloons around while music plays. When the music stops, the leader will call out one of the children's names. That child will read the Scripture address that is on his or her balloon. The child who has been working on that verse can take the opportunity to say the verse for the rest of the children. (The other children can sit on the floor for a few moments while this takes place.) If the child is successful at saying the entire passage, he or she can pop the balloon that has his or her address on it. There will be fewer balloons in play for each round.

MAKE A REBUS

Needed:

- large pieces of art paper

Give each child a large piece of art paper. Beforehand, with a pencil, lightly draw lines across each piece of paper. The lines should be about 4" apart. Children need this kind of guideline because they haven't yet developed a good sense of size and proportion. They will take part of the Scripture they have memorized and make a rebus, using pictures to portray as many of the words as possible, then filling in between the pictures with actual words. Give them a sample when you present the instructions. The pictures they substitute for words only have to make sense to them.

Introduce Key to Memorization #5

Talk with the kids about Key to Memorization #5—Share What You've Learned. It is important to find opportunities to share the Scripture that you have committed to memory. This will help cement it in your memory because saying it to someone else is totally different than saying it to yourself. You'll be motivated by the reaction you get from the people hearing it. And, it may just encourage someone else to start a holy habit of Scripture memorization.

VIDEOTAPE EVERYONE

Try to set up a videotape station for every four children. A prompter should sit next to the person videotaping with a copy of the Scripture, in case the child needs a little assistance. Encourage the children to cheer for each other and applaud when the videotaping is over.

CELEBRATE!

- Do something to celebrate.

- Go to a fast food restaurant together

- Have a build-your-own pizza party

- Invite everyone to your house for movie night and popcorn

- Go to a bounce party facility

- List the kids and the passages they memorized in the church information piece (newsletter, Facebook page, web site)

Meet with your worship leader and give him or her a list of the Scriptures the kids have memorized. Arrange for the kids to present their Scripture passages to the congregation, when that passage goes along with the theme of the service. When it fits for a particular service, he or she will notify you and you can refresh the child's memory verse. The worship leader may prefer to use the video sessions, but they're not quite as powerful as having the child live on the church platform. This is not mandatory for the kids, and you need to make it clear that this is only an option, if they would like to share in this way.

Here are some suggestions for longer passages to memorize. It's by no means an exhaustive list, and the best Scripture passages to memorize are the ones that are personally chosen, but this gives you a place to start.

Psalm 1

Psalm 8

Psalm 95:1-7

Psalm 100:1-5

Psalm 103:8-14

Psalm 139:7-14

Matthew 6:25-34

John 3:14-21

Romans 5:1-11

Romans 8:31-39

Romans 10:9-15

Romans 12:9-18

1 Corinthians 13:1-13

2 Corinthians 3:17—4:2

2 Corinthians 4:16-18

Galatians 6:7-10

Ephesians 3:16-21

Ephesians 6:10-18

Philippians 2:3-11

Philippians 4:4-9

Colossians 3:12-17

1 Peter 2:1-12

1 Peter 4:7-11

2 Peter 1:3-11

1 John 4:16-21

Notes: